LETTERS TO LEONARDO

THE TRUTH CHANGES EVERYTHING

DEE WHITE

Mazo Publishers

Letters To Leonardo
ISBN: 978-1-946124-55-5
Copyright © 2019 Dee White

Contact The Author
www.deescribe.com.au
Also via Dee White Author
on Facebook, Twitter and Instagram.

Mazo Publishers
P.O. Box 10474 ~ Jacksonville, FL 32247 USA

Website: www.mazopublishers.com
Email: mazopublishers@gmail.com

Bookstores
www.mazopub.com
www.au.mazopub.com (Australia)

⸗ℰ⸚

Letters To Leonardo is a fictional story,
inspired by real characters and events,
and is written in Australian English style.

⸗ℰ⸚

Cover Designer – Tania McCartney
Background by freecreatives.com

To the great Leonardo da Vinci,

Why am I writing to a dead guy?

a) My History teacher Mrs D says I have to.
b) Mrs D is dumb enough to think that somebody IMPORTANT and DEAD would want to know about me and my boring life.
c) Mrs D is a pain and this is her craziest homework suggestion yet.
d) All of the above.

Leonardo, if you guessed d), go to the top of the class – but don't expect to find me there. I don't have your greatness. Must admit though, when it comes to painting, I sure wish I did.

Matt, the not so great.

Hey Leonardo,

I'm on a roll. This is my second letter in two days! Mrs D will be shocked.

So why did I choose you, Leo (if I may)? Apart from the painting connection, there is the fact that you are someone I've actually heard of – I mean, who hasn't?

I'll tell you about my life, Leo – if that's what Mrs D wants. But they probably won't be the sort of letters she's expecting. I don't do furry pets and family holidays – probably comes from growing up without a mum.

Tomorrow's my birthday. I guess I could tell you about that.

Matt

Chapter One

My fifteenth birthday doesn't start out as anything special. Dad has to work. So what's new?

"We'll do something on my day off," he promises.

I guess it's natural to think of your dead Mum on your birthday. I try to remember her voice, but I can't. Was it low and soft, or one of those high-pitched, on-the-edge voices – one that goes up at the end of a sentence? Did she suffer in the accident – or was it quick? BANG! Like a falling tree?

Dad's about to load his mouth with cornflakes.

"What sort of car was Mum driving?" I ask.

He just about chokes on his breakfast. After he stops coughing, he puts down his spoon, and pastes on his sad face. "A Cortina – an old white one." Dad lays one hand on my shoulder, and uses the other to point out the window. "She's up there, keeping an eye on us – she'd be really proud of how you've grown up."

Seriously? I shove him away. "She's not a star, she's dead."

"You used to like it when I told you she was watching over you."

A snort bursts out of me. "I believed in Santa Claus back then."

Dad hands over his present. It's heavy and square, and it's wrapped in silver paper with cheery gold "Happy Birthdays" all over it.

It's a book on motorbikes. Just what I *didn't* want! I asked for painting lessons. There's this guy at the art shop in town – Steve Bridges – man, can he paint. And he has weekend classes. I took one of my pictures to him once. "You've got natural talent," he said. "Just need to learn about technique and composition."

"Thanks, Dave."

I drop the book on the kitchen table and turn back to my toast.

Dad shakes his head. The muscle at the corner of his eye

twitches and his mouth sets in a hard line, like he's trying not to react. "I know you wanted art lessons," he says, "but trust me, mate, art's a dead end career."

I take my plate and half-eaten toast to the sink, open the window and hurl my crusts to the birds. "What about Leonardo da Vinci?"

"He did a lot of other things as well. You can't make a good living out of painting." Dad sighs.

"And you can make a good living out of what *you* do?"

Dad's eye muscle twitches. "We manage."

I wind my foot around the chair leg and pull at the torn edges of the tablecloth. "You think?"

"We always have food on the table."

"Yeah, well I'd rather paint and starve, than do some lame real estate job."

I know I'm going too far but I can't seem to stop myself. Why won't he let me paint? I grab my present and the pile of birthday cards from relatives we never see, and take off to my room. I always read the letters in private – stops Dad from making his "secret admirer" jokes.

When I toss the book onto my bed, it misses and thuds on the floor. I leave it there, its pages sprawled out like the wings of a damaged moth. The cards lined up on my desk are from the usual suspects – Aunt Alexa, Nana Rose et cetera, and there's an envelope with writing I don't recognise and no return address.

Matthew Hudson, my name is in purple, loopy letters with feathered ends – as if the ink ran. Oversweet perfume drifting out of the envelope makes me shudder. I'm looking through a cloud, seeing a vague outline of a shape that I can almost recognise. My stomach jolts, as if all this means something – something important – but I don't know what.

I lay the card on the bed. The pulsing in my stomach won't go away. In my mind I escape to the world on the front of the card: Uluru at dusk, a blast of red and purple light. There's something about the painting that looks familiar.

The colours, that's it – they're just the sort of colours I would use. I trace my fingers over the brushstrokes, wondering if I'll ever be that good. Steve Bridges reckons I could be.

I turn the card over and look inside. That's when I nearly throw up.

To my darling Matt,
I don't expect you to understand why I'm sending this. I'm not even sure I do. I think about you every day. Not one of your birthdays goes by without me wishing I could see and hold you in my arms.
It gets harder every year.
I promised I wouldn't do this, but you're fifteen now – old enough to make your way in the world – old enough to know your mother.
You never stopped being the brightest star in my universe.
Have a wonderful birthday, darling boy.
Love Mum

It can't be from Mum – she's dead! Dave told me how she died. Who would do such a pathetic thing? Who would go to the trouble to drop a letter like that on me on my birthday? Who hates me that bad?

I read the words more carefully, but they don't change. A photo falls out when I shake the envelope. It's a picture of Mum and me – when I was about five – just before she "died".

This can't be right. It doesn't make sense. The letter *has* to be from her. Goosebumps creep up my arms and wash over my neck. My eyes sting and the memories splash together like a contaminated palette. I can't stop shivering. Can you have a heart attack and die of shock at fifteen?

I stare at the photo for ages, not believing. But it has to be true. You just have to look at us – we're replicas: same dimple on the chin, same questioning brown eyes. Mum! The card is definitely from Mum. My absent mother, where has she been for most of my life?

7

Chapter Two

I fight the urge to confront Dave, throw ten years of deceit in his face, now – trap him in his own lies. But what's the point? How do I know he'll tell me the truth *this* time?

Right now, I just want to smash something – him!

"Bye, Matt. Have a good day. I'll bring home pizza." The front door slams.

White-hot anger gouges a hole inside me. He's still pretending everything's normal. Course he is. He doesn't know that I know. Mum isn't dead!

I fling open the door to Dave's bedroom, tear open the top drawer of his old timber chest and rummage through it, scattering neat piles of socks and undies everywhere.

There has to be something here, something about Mum. But I don't know her. Don't even know what I'm looking for. I throw open the wardrobe door and ransack Dave's shelves. I toss neatly folded shirts and tank tops everywhere. I'm frantic, out of control, like a bat searching a cave exit that's been sealed off. I bang my arm on a broken corner of the shelf. Ouch. I keep on searching but find nothing.

Under the shelves is another nest of drawers. I tug the first drawer open, fierce so the handle pulls off. I drop it on the floor and kick it under the bed.

Finally, in the drawer with the missing handle, there's something: a small ivory bible with Zara Templeton in neat calligraphy on the inside front cover. That must have been who she was before she became a Hudson. Inside the bible is a wedding photo of a much younger Dave with thick, red-blond hair. With Mum. Of course it's her. She wears a light purple dress with lipstick to match. Not the white wedding dress you see in movies. Her hair's as black as a starless sky.

I hold the bible in my hand, close my eyes and try to remember. But I can't. What did her feet sound like on the kitchen floor in the morning? Did her clothes rustle when she walked? Was her sneeze soft and quick like a cat or loud and wet like Dave's? Did she only wear perfume when she went out, or was there the hint of her that lingered wherever she went? Why has Dave done this to me? Why did he keep me from my own mother? Why didn't *she* write a return address on the envelope?

My shoulders sag. There's a lump in my throat, but my eyes are dry. Ten years of tears that I can't cry. The anger won't let me. It forces me on, forces me to keep searching for the truth. Where's mum? Why did she leave?

I drag out the next drawer. Nothing. And the next. Still nothing. I wrench the bottom drawer out, have just enough control left not to throw the whole thing through Dave's window. Savagely, I thrust my hand in amongst the shorts and swimwear. Something pricks my finger. It's some sort of pin with two owls at the blunt end. Don't really know what it's for, but it says *Mayberry Girls' Grammar* across the bottom. Girls' Grammar, it can't belong to Dave.

Standing in the pile of Dave's clothes feels good. I love that they're not neat folded stacks any more. They're a twisted mess like my insides.

I have a mum – and she's not dead! I want to prick every single finger with the Mayberry Girls' Grammar pin, wipe the blood on Dave's white business shirts, then watch him freak. See how he handles shock! I want the sting of ten bleeding fingers to distract me from the pain that's coming from deep in my chest. Too bad I'm such a wimp.

I kick the wardrobe where Dave hangs his suits. The door vibrates, but doesn't show the mark of my fury.

Each suit hangs next to its matching shirt and tie, all coat hangers facing the same way. So neat and pathetic. I take every piece of clothing from its hanger and put them *all* back out of order, mismatched. Put his purple jacket with pale pink pants, a blue shirt with green paisley tie. I arrange everything into a confused jumble, and scoop up the bible, photo and hatpin. It all fits easily in my back pocket. All that's left to show my mother even existed. It's like Dave tried to wipe her from his memory, and this stuff was accidentally left behind.

Back in my room, I lay Mum's stuff out on my desk; between the watercolour pencils that were last year's birthday present from Troy, and a pile of scrap paper sketchpads. I take out the photo she sent. My hand's shaking too much to hold it steady.

When I think about it, I'm so angry with her I want to rip the photo up. What's her game? But there's part of me that always wanted a mother, wishes I could use the image to bring her back. Sitting on my bed, clutching the photo to my chest doesn't make the pain go away.

There's so much I don't know. We look kind of the same, but what else connects us? What sort of music does she listen to? Does she go to bed late too? Why don't I know this about my own mother? With each question, the anger pounds harder in my chest, clangs like a church bell. I look out my bedroom window and wonder, can anyone else hear? If I lifted up my shirt, could they see the gaping hole in my heart?

Of all the things I found that belong to her, the only one that's any use is the Mayberry Girls' Grammar pin. At least that tells me where she went to school. I slam myself down on my chair in front of my computer, shove the mouse towards my browser and click. My fingers stumble on the keys. "Mayberry Girls' Grammar." Finally, on the third try, the screen signals "Website found".

My stomach churns when the home page loads. What do I do now? Where do you start searching for someone that you shouldn't need to be looking for? Salt stings my eyes. I tap out Zara Hudson. The screen taunts "no match". Thanks for nothing! I'm about to flick the "off" switch, when I realise ... she wouldn't be Zara Hudson. She wasn't married then!

"Don't stop now," says the white-hot anger.

She has to be here! I have to find out *something* about her – there has to be more. There has to be more substance to her than what was in Dave's cupboard. Who was she friends with? Is there *someone* who knew her, someone who can tell me the truth, someone who might even know where she is now?

I type in Tara Zempleton – "nothing". Oops. I tap the keys hard and retype. Finally, there she is: "Z Templeton" typed underneath the class photo, "Class of 81". She's four years younger than Dave.

School Captain for that year is listed as K Armain. I don't know if she was friends with Mum or not, but she was in her class. And there's an email listing, as good as an invitation. Perhaps "K Armain" might know stuff about the mysterious, long-lost Miss Templeton – absent mother of Matt Hudson who turned fifteen today.

"Happy Birthday and have a fun day". That was the pathetic inscription inside Dave's card. Are we having fun yet? NO!

I wish the pounding in my chest would stop – now my head's thumping as well. I can't believe this, any of it. What am I going to say to her – to this Armain person? I know I should take time to try and calm myself, think what to do next, but anger is pushing me forward. I can't stop now. If I stop, all of this will come down on me like an avalanche, and I'll be left in a snow cave with barely enough air to breathe.

I key in her address: karmain@motoona.com. My fingers are staccato on the keys.

Hi,

You don't know me, but I'm the son of Zara Templeton, who ran out on me when I was five *(Delete that last bit.)*

I haven't seen my mother for ten years. I need to find her because my lying father isn't likely to be any help. *(Delete that too.)*

I'm hoping that you, or someone else who went to school with Mum, might know where she is and why she took off. *(Delete again.)*. It's really important that I contact her.

"What makes you think she'd want to hear from you?" says a voice in my head. *(Delete all of that.)*

I start again. I end up with:

Hi,

I'm Matt Hudson.

You went to school with my mum, Zara Templeton.

I haven't seen her for ten years and am trying to track her down.

Can you help?

Thanks,

Matt Hudson

I press "send", and break into a cold sweat, just make it to the toilet in time to heave up breakfast.

All day, I wait, holding the photo to my chest. No food, no school. I sit on my bed, trying to block out words that echo over and over in my mind as if someone keeps pressing, "rewind": *You're fifteen now ... old enough to know your mother.* Over and over and over!

My mother is not dead! The truth of it fries my brain.

Hey Leonardo,

Parents ride you for every little white lie – then you find out they've told you the whopper of all whoppers – and kept it up for the last ten years.

Happy Birthday, Matt, oh and by the way, YOUR MOTHER IS NOT DEAD!

So, Leo, that's how my birthday went. Can't even begin to tell you what's going on in my head. This time, I'm not writing for Mrs D, I'm writing for me. Have to let it out somehow. And it's not like there's anyone who's alive NOW, who I can actually trust. Maybe writing this down might help me make sense of everything.

Who knows, you might even write back. Seems like dead people do send letters.

Matt

Chapter Three

The bedroom door bursts open. Dave stands gaping at me. "Oh my God, Matt. We've been robbed. Are you okay? They didn't hurt you?"

As if anyone could hurt me more than you have!

My laugh is dry like the crackle of sunburnt bracken. "I'm fine, Dave. Never been better." The lie moves up through my body and collects in my throat in bubbles of hysteria. Suddenly, I burst out laughing and can't stop: loud, high-pitched, hysterical giggles.

"Matt, are you sure you're all right?"

It makes me laugh more. I can't stop.

"For God's sake, Matt, what's wrong with you?"

That's the slap in the face I needed. "What's wrong with *me*? That's a joke."

I shove Dave out of the room and slam the door shut. I'd lock it but we don't have locks on our doors. Dave has always said we don't need them – that we don't have anything to hide from each other. *Huh! As if.*

Pushing my double bed up against the door so he can't get back in, I jam my finger between the bedhead and the wall. It's the same finger I pricked with the Mayberry Girls' Grammar pin. The pain brings me back to where all this started – with Dave's lies.

He knocks relentlessly on the door. "Talk to me, Matt."

I don't answer.

"You can't stay in there forever."

Says who?

Finally, his retreating footsteps clomp on the wooden floorboards. Now there's no sound except my breath coming in short angry wheezes. I need to calm down, but I can't. The anger is all that's keeping me from completely losing it.

No answer on my computer screen from K Armain, no explanation for any of this.

The smell of pizza wafts under my door and I realise how hungry I am. It's making me dizzy. I check the emails one last time – still nothing! I push my bed back to its usual place and open the bedroom door.

Dave eyes me off when I walk into the kitchen, as if he's working out what sort of mood I'm in and how to handle me. He dumps a huge slab of ham and pineapple pizza in front of me and asks, "How was school, Matt?"

He's going for the "let's pretend nothing happened" approach. Why am I not surprised? Because I've just found out *that's* what he's been doing for most of my life.

"Didn't go to school. Didn't feel like it." I glare at him, dare him to give me a hard time over it.

Dave sighs. He's watching me intently, as if he just figured out who the burglar was. "Education is important, you know." He passes a glass of lime cordial.

So is being honest with your kid.

I take a huge bite of pizza.

We're like two cows in a paddock; the only sound is the chewing of pizza. The food helps the nausea, but not the pounding anger. I want to confront him. Now. But I can't stomach the thought of more lies.

Dave takes his empty plate to the sink. "So, why didn't you go to school?"

When I keep munching, he moves next to me. "Should I call the police, Matt? Were we burgled or do you know something about what happened in my room?"

I shrug.

Dave's voice is firm. "Matt, what do you know?"

When I stand and shove my chair against the table, cordial spills everywhere.

"What do *I* know?"

Dave nods.

"That the mess in your room is nowhere near as crappy as my life." I'm only just keeping it together.

"Matt? What's wrong? What's happened?"

14

Dave's breath is warm on my face. I step away and press my lips together tight, not ready to answer questions yet, or even to ask my own. I need to know more about Mum first – from an authentic source. I need to know that what Dave tells me isn't MORE LIES.

He goes to the bookcase. I roll my eyes, wait for him to pull down *Sons and the Single Parent*, by Frank Rosenbaum. That's where he goes for advice when he's under pressure. It's his bible. Dave's always quoting, according to Rosenbaum. It's crap. "A good father is his son's best friend." That's one of his favourites. Dave told someone that once, that we were best buddies and didn't need a woman stuffing things up for us.

That's his opinion, not mine. I never had a say in it.

"What are you looking for, Dave?"

He's about to reach for the book when he stops, turns and stares at me, his head tipped to the side as if he's trying to read me, to understand what all this is about.

"What do you do when your son gives you attitude? Better ask Rosenbaum, Dave."

In my room, I slam the door and push my bed back up against it.

There's still nothing from K Armain.

I stare at my *Mona Lisa* screen saver, wondering why I chose that out of all Leo's paintings. Tears sting my eyes. Was she *ever* a mother? Did she have a son?

Questions! So many questions – and no answers.

I trace my fingers over the smooth forehead of Mona Lisa. What was Leonardo thinking when he painted her? What's that "air of mystery" all about?

It's too much. My brain feels like it's going to burst. Somehow I have to push this out of my mind, at least until I know more. But I don't know how to stop thinking about it. Maybe delving into someone else's life, might make the wait for information about my own more bearable. I Google "Leonardo da Vinci".

_____

Hey Leonardo,

Talk about serendipity. Just found out it would have been your birthday today too.

Seems we have a bit in common. Your dad took you away from your mum. How weird is that? How did you deal with the missing bits in your life?

I'm struggling, have to admit.

I've always felt like an unfinished painting, and now I'm starting to understand why. Always felt like a background wash, with just an outline and all the important detail left out.

So much of me is Dave, but so much is different. Like my art, and the way I like being by myself.

Dave hates the quiet. Has to have people and action. Maybe it helps him forget who he really is, what he's done.

Matt

_____

Still no email! It's killing me!

Leo has this one painting, *St Jerome.* I can't stop looking at it, at the torture in the saint's eyes. He's crouching among these craggy rocks, prostrate before that open-mouthed lion. That painting right there, that's everything that's going on inside me. Wish I had half Leonardo's talent, and balance. Everything's in proportion (except the right hand's a bit big) but hell, nobody's perfect.

Even Dave, especially Dave with his self-help books, and his "honest real estate agent" face. Good old honest Dave, his truth is scratchy at best.

Come on K Armain! Where are you? Answer my email!

Hey Leo,

Did you miss your mum? Did you ever wonder in those years you never saw her, what she really looked like, not just in photos, I mean. Then again, you probably didn't even have photos back then.

Did it bother you, going to live with your dad, or were you too young just like me? Kids never get a say in stuff like that.

Women, you painted heaps of them. Was that how you got over losing your mum? Do you ever get over something like that?

Maybe that's what I need, to get out my gear and start painting. Thanks for the tip, Leo.

Matt

I lie on my bed, eyes closed, trying to work it all out. Until now, I never really thought about who I was, or where I came from.

Dave never talked about Mum, except to say she was killed in that car accident. We moved soon after she "died" and our relatives live miles away. There's never been anyone I could talk to who knew Mum. I guess I should have thought that was strange. But it was just the way things were.

When I was seven I asked Dave if I was like her and it really fired him up. "You're not like your mother, and never will be!" He seemed so mad that I was too scared to ask what he meant.

Sometimes I used to wonder what it would be like to have a mum at parent-teacher night or helping out in the school canteen. But I always told myself, "Forget it, she's dead. It's never going to happen."

But it could have. Mum could have taken me to school and watched my music concerts, if she'd known about them.

She's not dead!

Hey Leonardo,

Do you reckon it's possible that Mum and Dave agreed to this between them? Maybe she didn't want me!

But what did she say in her card? "She thinks about me every day" – like she misses me. Like none of this was her choice.

What else haven't I been told? Is Dave that warped he just wants to keep me for himself? Heaps of kids in my class live with their mums and spend weekends and holidays with their dads. Why couldn't we have lived like that? Why did he wipe her from our lives altogether?

Dave's a scammer. What you see is not what you get. He's like a picture that's been painted over. When you scrape off the surface layers you find the real hypocritical, lying Dave. I hate him.

He's going to feel my pain.

They say the pen is mightier than the sword, but what about the paintbrush, or the spray can? No pathetic little sketchpads for you. You painted big and bold. I could do over Dave's bedroom bright orange. He'd hate that.

But my artwork is going where everyone can see, something massive, a masterpiece.

Going to paint something immense like your Last Supper. Can't believe it's nearly nine metres long. Now that's some canvas.

I know just the place for my public exhibition.

Matt

I fall asleep at the laptop with the *Mona Lisa* screen saver watching over me. When I wake up it's still not light. My computer screen tells me it's 3.48 am. I've been slumped over with my head on the keyboard, and my neck aches. It feels like it has been stretched between two trees. The crushing feeling in my chest is still there, and my legs have been squashed for way too long under the computer desk.

Still no email from K Armain! I slam the keyboard with my fist.

There's too much going on in my head for me to sleep again, too much to find out, too much to think about. There are too many things boiling away inside me.

I stand and stretch to get my legs working again and to loosen the tightness in my neck and shoulders. Then I sit back at the computer to wait for morning.

At 8.00 am the front door slams as Dave leaves for work. He hasn't even knocked on my door. Rosenbaum probably told him to leave me alone – pretend we didn't argue, wait for me to make the first move. *That's not going to happen.*

My laptop beeps "incoming mail". Finally, it's there, in my inbox, something from Kathryn Armain. I stare at it, too scared to click "open". What if she tells me to mind my own business? Or worse?

My eyes are heavy from not enough sleep. I want to throw up again. "Don't be such a wimp," I tell myself. "This is what you've been waiting for." I have to focus to make my fingers click on Kathryn Armain's reply. My stomach churns as I read each word carefully to make sure I get it right.

Dear Matt,

Sorry I can't give you the information you need.

I have spoken to a couple of girls from our class, but we lost contact with your mother after high school. Bethany Summers remembers seeing something about her in the paper about ten years ago, but can't remember what it was. Could have been her art. She was a fantastic painter.

Your mother went out with a guy called Scott Reesborough from Ashton High. You might find his details on their website. He could have kept in touch.

Hope you find her.

All the best,

Kathryn Armain

Chapter Four

Mum's an artist! Dave forgot to mention that too! Is that why he doesn't like me doing art?

She paints! Like me!

It connects me to her – makes me feel excited, hopeful. But I don't even know where she is. Kathryn's email gave me nothing. I go from hyped to gutted in a blink. My stomach rumbles, reminding me it's breakfast time, but I'm too worked up to eat.

In the living room, I lie on the couch, drinking milk straight from the bottle. Pity Dave's not here to see me.

The doorbell rings. I ignore it, but it keeps ringing. As I amble down the hallway, the front door opens. Dave mustn't have locked it, probably thought I'd be leaving straight after him.

It's not Dave, it's my best mate, Troy. He walks in wearing a stethoscope around his neck made from a shoelace and two round cupboard door knobs. "Dr Daly at your service." He's carrying a huge tub of chocolate ice-cream – the best.

"What are you doing?" I can't help laughing.

"Your dad let you take a day off school! Thought there must be a medical emergency."

I rotate in front of him. "As you can see, there isn't."

Troy puts the ice-cream behind his back. "So you don't need Dr Daly's magic remedy?"

I wrestle the tub from him. I'm at least ten centimetres taller than Troy, so it's not that hard.

He gives in easily. "You might as well have it. Happy Birthday for yesterday."

The ice-cream has a twenty dollar art supply voucher taped to the lid. Now that's a proper present.

"Thanks a lot, man." In the kitchen I grab two spoons, and hand one to Troy. "Help yourself."

Troy screws up his nose. "Chocolate ice-cream this early?"

"Why not?"

He shrugs, takes a spoonful and shovels it into his mouth. "My olds wouldn't let me eat this sort of stuff for breakfast."

"Yeah, well, my old isn't here."

Troy shifts in his seat. "So, how was your birthday?"

I jam the lid back on the ice-cream and shove it in the freezer. "We'll be late for school if we don't hurry."

Troy slips his stethoscope into his backpack and follows me out the door. "Where were you yesterday?"

"Where were you?"

Troy scratches his head. "At school."

"I didn't see you there." I slam the front door shut.

Troy looks so confused it's hard for me to keep a straight face. "*You* weren't at school," he says.

"Yes, I was." I lope off down the road. "You must have been too preoccupied with Tina Armstrong to notice."

Troy takes off after me. "She is a bit distracting."

"What are you doing after school tonight?"

Troy breathes hard as he tries to keep up. "What do you want to do?"

I wait for him catch me. "Outdoor art."

"Cool. I'm in."

Everyone needs a best mate like Troy – up for anything. Doesn't ask questions, just goes with it. We arrange to meet back at his house after school. I have to go home first to get my supplies.

I grab two mouthfuls of chocolate ice-cream and race out carrying a box of spray cans.

Troy's sister Angie stares at me when I walk in the door, but she doesn't say anything. Troy already has his gear stashed in his backpack. I've always gone for the box option, ever since a red can leaked and it looked like I'd decapitated a small animal in my pack.

Troy points out the door. "To the water tank." He gallops down the driveway like a pretend medieval knight. I run after him. In spite of the fury bubbling and seething inside me since yesterday, Troy makes me laugh – always has.

The water tank's at the top of Mather's Hill. It's a hard climb, especially carrying a cardboard box full of spray cans.

Troy nudges me with his pack. "So, how come you wagged?"

Still not ready to tell him, I grip the box tighter, and clamber onwards. "You shouldn't have to go to school on your birthday."

Troy punches me on the shoulder. "Yeah, I reckon you're right."

The water tank pokes out the top of the hill. Apart from Mather's Hill, Brabham is completely flat. From up here, you can see houses dotted everywhere like hundreds and thousands on a piece of fairy bread. The river runs through them like treacle. That's our other favourite place to hang out – at the biggest waterhole on the river, where the rope swing used to be – the place where we chill out in summer.

We dump our paints on the ground about five metres from the water tank where we can view our whole canvas.

"What are we doing here?" Troy has a yellow can in his hand.

"Painting."

"Why?"

I want to tell him about Mum, but how do you bring up a subject like that, out of the blue? Do you start with the first lie or the last one? How do you say that your dad has kept your mum from you all your life? How do you do it without crying? It's too big, for now! I swallow it back inside.

The can is smooth and cool against my face. I love the smell of paint – and being in control. It's hard to do fine work, but cans have impact. And that's what I'm going for. I paint flames, licking up over the top of the concrete tank.

"Awesome," says Troy.

I stand back to look. "Yeah, but it needs more detail."

Troy picks up a can of green from my box and puts a sharper nozzle on it. He shows me how to etch around the orange with quick, firm strokes. It's all in the can control and knowing which colour and nozzle to use. Now the flames look even more brilliant against the green. With each stroke, a small piece of anger seeps out through my fingertips.

"So, who did you pick for your History assignment?" asks Troy. "Michelangelo?"

"Close, Leonardo da Vinci. What about you?"

Troy makes his eyes bulge and walks stiff-legged towards me. "I was thinking of Frankenstein ... the monster ... not the doctor."

I back away. "He wasn't a real person."

Troy says in a deep robot-like voice, "How do you know?" He falls on the ground, laughing and I drop down next to him.

"Has Mrs D given the okay?"

Troy winks at me. "No, but I'll talk her into it."

"Do you reckon she'll go for Leonardo?"

Troy nods. "Course she will. He's perfect – he's famous, real and dead."

I laugh. "And awesome! I've been finding out all sorts of stuff about him."

Troy picks up a can of paint, lid still on, and aims it at me. "Is that why you wagged yesterday – to do your homework? You must have been sick."

Laughing, I get to my feet. The painted water tank looks awesome. It's wild having such a huge canvas. "Wish we were around in Leo's day?"

"No TVs or computers!"

"Yeah, I know. But it would have been cool to have a canvas as big as a ceiling or the whole wall of a building."

"Those flames are awesome." Troy grins. "You have serious talent."

"Pity Dave doesn't agree." Just thinking about him paints my anger red, makes it burn bright again. I reach for the black can.

"What are you doing now?" Troy puts out a hand to stop me.

I sidestep him, shake the paint and take off the lid.

Troy raises an eyebrow. "Don't do any more, Matt. Don't wreck it."

I lift the can. "Too late." I point the nozzle and spray in massive letters across the flames, *Dave Hudson is a liar!*

Hey Leonardo,

See how you inspired me?

Truth is important in art, don't you think?

Truth is important. full stop.

Matt

Nobody in this town (except Steve Bridges) seems to appreciate art.

At 7 pm I find Scott Reesborough's email address on the Ashton High website.

At 7.05 Brabham's head police officer, Constable Huggins, knocks on my door, blasts me with garlic breath and asks me to "accompany him to the police station". He could have said, "Come to Mars with me," and I reckon I would have gone. Can't make myself care about anything.

Brabham Police Station is like an old farmhouse – could have been the first thing ever built in the town. The ancient wooden floors creak and sag when you walk on them. Now there's a building that needs a paint job.

The first thing I notice inside the place is garlic. That's what the inside of the cop car smells like. That's the odour that drapes over PC Huggins like a cloak. It's not just his breath. It oozes out of his skin like invisible sap.

Troy's there, juggling mints, when I arrive. He's getting pretty good; he can juggle three mints in one hand for about two minutes without dropping any. He tosses two up high, catches them in his mouth and crunches down hard.

I move to sit next to him, but another police officer steps

between us. "If you'll come this way, Mr Hudson," she says.

Where's Dave? Then I realise she's actually talking to me. She shows me to an office with glass windows.

"Take a seat." She pulls out a black chair for herself, and indicates for me to sit across the desk from her. "Your friend confessed to the vandalism of the water tank," she says, "but we think there's more to it."

At that moment PC Huggins walks in, breathing garlic all over us.

The female PC's mobile phone rings, and she goes out to take the call, leaving me and Huggins alone.

"It wasn't Troy, it was me," I say.

"We know. A witness saw you in action." PC Huggins fixes me with a look that clearly states, 'I'm not impressed'.

Yeah well he's not the only one. I slouch back in my chair.

Dave's Mazda grinds to a halt out the front of the police station. I'd recognise those squeaky bearings anywhere.

PC Huggins gets to his feet. "I'll be back."

"Okay, Arnie," I mumble under my breath as the PC's large blue butt disappears out the door.

He comes back wearing a scowl like a bear in a nest of bees, and Dave follows him into the office.

Dave stands, one hand on his hip, the other resting on the table right next to me. "Why, Matt? What did you think you were doing?"

I'm so mad, I can't even look at him.

What was *I* doing?

Dave moves closer and puts his hand on my shoulder. I shrug it off.

"Why, mate?" he asks.

I'm not his 'mate'. I'm not one of his real estate clients to be smarmed by his "honest Dave" impersonation. I push his arm away and square up with him. "Why not?"

He takes a step back. "Matt, what's got into you? You're fifteen now, I'd expect a bit more maturity."

"Oh, that's right, I had a birthday this week, didn't I?" I lean back in my chair so that the front legs come off the ground.

He hates that.

He pushes the chair back down again. "I'm sorry I had to work and we haven't got around to doing anything yet."

"Yeah, Dave."

Dave pulls out a chair and sits next to me. "Is that what this is about? You're mad at me for working on your birthday?"

I roll my eyes. "Yeah, right."

"This is serious, Matt. These are the sorts of stupid pranks that can wreck a person's life."

"Mine's stuffed already."

"Matt!" PC Huggins and Dave say it in unison.

My life *is* stuffed. Everything I ever thought to be true isn't. My life's a lie.

Dave looks smug. "People only use words like 'stuffed' because they're not literate enough to think of a better way to express themselves."

I'm sick of his crap. "Whatever." I stand up and fling the chair against the wall.

"If that's your attitude, you'd better wait outside while I speak with Constable Huggins," Dave says.

"You do that!" I slam the door behind me.

Troy has left the police station already. His parents must have come and got him. I wander the corridors, trying to block out the murmur of the PC and Dave talking. I don't want to know. I study the noticeboards of all the "most wanted" and "missing" people. So where's the poster for Zara Hudson? My mother! Why isn't it hanging there too?

I smell the PC before I see him. "Your father and I have come to an agreement," he says.

Dave sits with arms folded.

"I'm going to let you off with a warning, this time," says PC.

Big deal!

"Your father has agreed to pay to get the tank resprayed."

"Why? My artwork's better than what was there."

The PC leans towards me. "And your artwork is a criminal offence."

And what about lying to your kid for ten years? What sort of offence is that?

Dave stands. "We'll be going then, Constable Huggins. Thanks for your understanding. I'm sure this won't happen again."

Don't bet on it.

As soon as we walk through the front door of our house, Dave starts. "Why did you do it, Matt? I've always been on the level with you?"

I slam the door shut behind us. He has to be kidding!

"What's with the *Dave Hudson is a liar*? Why would you write something like that?"

I just about choke on my words. "You figure it out." I bolt to my room, turn on my laptop, and key in Scott Reesborough's email address. I copy the message I sent to Kathryn Armain, paste it into the body of the email, delete the part about "going to school with Zara", and press "send". Dave knocks on my door at 9 pm and says, "We need to talk about today – properly. Are you ready?"

"No."

"If you're too tired to talk, you'd better put your light out and get some sleep." I can hear the carefully controlled anger in his voice. According to Rosenbaum, "A parent should never lose their cool in times of conflict."

"Fine!"

I turn off the light, but I don't sleep. Unanswered questions about Mum swirl around in my head then disappear into blackness.

Chapter Five

When the alarm goes off I leap out of bed to check my emails. Nothing from Scott. I sit for ages, staring at the screen – trying to "will" a message to come through. After a while everything goes out of focus. I let my mind wander through the information maze that's been scrambling my brain ever since I read that letter, wonder if I'll ever find my way out.

Dave opens the bedroom door. "What are you doing, Matt? It's time for school and you haven't even had breakfast."

I move to block his view of the laptop screen. "I'll grab some fruit before I go."

"Make sure you do. You need to eat properly. Rosenbaum says junk food's the worst thing for a growing body."

He would, wouldn't he? "Don't worry about me, Dave. You don't want to be late for work."

"What's with this 'Dave' all the time?"

"What's with the 'Matt'?"

"It's your name."

"So? Dave is yours."

Dave throws up his hands. "I have an early appointment, but we'll talk when I get home."

Unlikely.

As soon as the front door slams, I go to the kitchen, shove three choc-coated muesli bars in my pack and race out the door, just in time to catch the bus.

At school everyone's talking about our water tank art. It's got a few of them asking questions about Dave too. Good.

First period is History. Just my luck! We're supposed to hand in our first two letters. Mine are done, but there's nothing I'm prepared to share just yet.

Somehow, Troy has talked Mrs D into letting him use Frankenstein as his "significant person", providing his letters meet the assignment criteria. We have to "demonstrate an understanding of what life was like for our 'subject' and tell them about our modern world."

First thing Mrs D does is call for volunteers to read out one of their pieces. Troy's hand shoots up.

"Teacher's pet," I whisper.

"Just sharing my talent," says Troy.

"Yeah, right. Trying to impress Tina Armstrong more like it."

"So?"

Mrs D interrupts. "Troy, seeing as you're the only volunteer, perhaps you'd like to start."

Troy takes his tablet to the front of the class. He stands in front of Mrs D's table. Troy winks at me and starts reading. His voice is loud and clear. He doesn't even look nervous.

"Dear Frankenstein (Don't mind if I call you Frankie, do you?), Like me, you were brilliant and misunderstood ..."

Brad Jenkins and Damon Knox groan.

"Poor Troy," Tina, teases.

Troy grins at her and keeps reading.

"Frankenstein wasn't even your name. They just called you that because that's who created you. Dr Victor Frankenstein ... But you were really, the Monster."

Troy rolls his R's for effect and Tina giggles.

"Overactor," I mouth at him.

He takes a bow.

"Please continue, Mr Daly." Mrs D is on her feet now.

Troy stands up straighter.

"Wouldn't like to have been in your lounge room, Frankie Monster. Apart from the fact you would have killed me or at the very least, caused me severe pain ..."

"I'll be causing you pain, Mr Daly, if you don't take this seriously."

"Sorry, Mrs D." Troy reads:

"I wouldn't have liked to have been in your lounge room because back in 1818, when you were created, there was no television, no computers, no devices."

"Man, how did people live back then?" says Brad.

Troy talks over the top of Brad.

"Wouldn't be able to build you today, Frankie. You can't just get your hands on body parts that easily. Need permission to do that sort of stuff. Anyway, thought I'd recreate you so you could see what life is really like for me. I made a Frankenstein mask and wore it around the house. Freaked out my little sister, Angie, so badly she had nightmares, and I've been banned from wearing your face any more."

"You don't need a mask. You're butt ugly anyway," Damon yells out.

The whole class erupts into laughter, including Troy. Even Mrs D has a wry smile.

"So, Mr Daly, what else do you think your 'historical character' needs to know about your life?"

Troy keeps reading.

"I wrote this letter on my tablet because that's what we use now instead of paper and pens. I guess people were pretty poor back in England in 1818, but we have plenty to eat where I live today. I live in a place called Brabham and go to Brabham High School and I have the coolest History teacher. Her name is Mrs D."

Brad and Damon make vomiting noises. I shake my head.

"Thank you, that will do, Mr Daly. Perhaps we'll hear from

31

someone else now."

Mrs D looks directly at me and I look down.

"How about you, Mr Hudson?"

"I'm still doing the research, Mrs D. There's heaps to learn about da Vinci's life."

"A week, Mr Hudson. You have a week. If your letters aren't to me by then, you'll have to do them in your lunch hour."

"Yes, Mrs D." I think about Troy's piece and a chuckle escapes.

"I don't think you're taking this seriously enough, Mr Hudson. You do want a pass in this subject, don't you?"

"A leave pass," Troy whispers.

I try not to laugh, but I can't stop myself. Troy cracks up too.

Mrs D's face goes red. "I've had it with you two disrupting my class." She glares at me. "Get out! Go and explain to Mr Madden why you haven't done your homework."

She's had it with me! "Whatever." I pick up my books and storm out the door. Troy grabs his gear and follows.

He races to catch up with me. Suddenly serious, he says, "What's with you lately?"

"Nothing."

Troy puts his hand on my shoulder. "You've been weird for days. One minute you're laughing, the next you're going off your nut."

"You wouldn't get it."

"Try me."

"No, thanks."

When we get to Madden's office, the door's closed. He's already got somebody with him.

"Stuff it," says Troy. "Perfect day for a swim."

It takes me back to when I was a kid and Dave was selling land near the ocean. If nobody was around he'd say, "Perfect day for a swim". And we'd go down the beach. I don't want to think about Dave. But I don't want to see Madden either. There are enough hassles in my life already.

"Let's go." I lope away from the headmaster's door.

Troy pats me on the back. "I can't believe it. You're wagging two days in the one week. Something has seriously got to you, hasn't it?"

"Maybe."

"What?"

"Nothing I can't figure out."

Troy punches me lightly on my arm. "Doesn't look like you're getting very far."

I slam my pack on the ground. "If I lived your perfect life, I'd probably think things were pretty funny too. But I don't."

"Settle."

"Forget the swim."

I run home, straight to my room where I turn on the computer.

Finally, there's an email from Scott Reesborough.

Matt,

Might have something for you. Would rather talk to you than email. Ring me on the number at the bottom of this email.

Scott

I pick up my phone and key in the number.

"Hello, this is Scott Reesborough. How can I help you?" says a deep voice.

I start shaking. This guy could be the missing link, the person that can help me find my mother. But what if he doesn't know anything? Then I'll be right back where I started. I suck in air. "Er ... Mr Reesborough. It's Matt ... Matt Hudson. I got your email."

"Call me Scott," he says. "I understand you're after information about your mother. I haven't seen her for a long time. Didn't know she'd married or had kids."

"Kid – there's just me, as far as I know."

Scott seems to hesitate as if he's not sure how much to say. "Matt, I don't know where your mother is," he says eventually.

It's in the hesitation. He knows more.

"Can you tell me anything about her that might help me find her?" I grip my phone tighter.

Scott pauses again. "She had some problems when I knew her."

Problems, what does he mean by problems? A dad like mine who lies, or worse? Is she in trouble with the law? Maybe she's been hurt in an accident? My head spins with all the possibilities. "What sort of problems?"

"I don't think it's really up to me to go into it. But she had some sort of breakdown after we finished school. She went away for a while. To a place called Barry Hill."

A breakdown! It's worse than I thought. What if there's something major wrong with her? "How come she went there?"

"It's a psychiatric hospital."

"Why?" A cloud of doubt settles around me. Do I really want to go here?

"I'm not sure what her problem was. She was always highly strung – artistic, you know. I saw her for a while after she came out of Barry Hill, then she moved away without telling me."

"How can I find her?"

"You could try Barry Hill. She might have gone back there at some stage. Or they might have some record of where she went. She was amazing, your mother – but not easy. Never easy."

I hang up slowly. I have somewhere to start looking, but it's petrifying. Why do people talk about Mum in the past tense, as if she really is dead?

Dave walks in around dinner time, just as I'm finishing off my last ham and cheese toasted sandwich. He stares at my empty plate and raises an eyebrow.

"I hope you had vegetables."

"The plate was covered in them."

"Good. Growing teens need to keep up their vitamins."

"Yes, Rosenbaum."

Dave frowns, pours himself a glass of water and sits down at the table. "I hope you realise that what you did at the water tank was wrong."

I refuse to even look at him. "Whatever."

"You can't go writing things like that about me in public. The whole town would have seen it."

"Good."

Dave clunks his glass on the table. "If you've got a grievance with me, let's deal with it here. You don't have to make it public."

I shrug and head to my room.

"Don't you care that you could have ruined my reputation?"

"You did that all by yourself."

I slam the door behind me.

The last thing I hear before I put the music up loud is Dave's plaintive voice. "We'll have to talk about this sooner or later."

Hey Leonardo,

This is the piece that Mrs D says I have to write to pass Year Nine History. So, here goes.

We wouldn't travel by cart from Vinci to Florence – like you did when you were my age. Where I live, the horse and mule have been made redundant as a form of transport. We drive cars, like the ones that you did plans and drawings for way back when. Today we build and ride in them.

Not being married mattered a lot more in your day. You could never be Ser Piero's heir because he wouldn't marry your mum. So he apprenticed you to Verrocchio, which ended up being a good choice. Your talent would have been seriously wasted if you never got to paint.

In my country, these days, people don't care if your parents are married or not. In fact, heaps of people don't even bother; they just live together.

At one time you lived with your grandparents and Uncle Francesco who farmed olives and grapes. We still farm them today. Who knows why? Olives taste bad.

You used to have heaps of marble masons and carpenters in your town. We don't have anybody in Brabham who builds out of stone, and the only carpenter is Ben McGraw who has never been quite the same since he fell off the church roof.

Matt

Hey Leonardo,

Here's what I really wanted to write.

You're dead so none of this is logically possible, but it feels like you get what I'm going through – like you understand.

Getting taken from your mum sucks. Bet they never fooled you with their lies though, Leo. You just have to look at your paintings to know, "There's someone who sees right to the heart of everything".

Wish Mum could have seen my water tank mural, and given me an artist's opinion.

If she walked through the door now, at least she'd be able to explain why she decided to opt out of my life for the last ten years. And it'd be good for me too. I'd be able to ask her all the stuff I need to know.

It was different for you, Leo. You went to live with your grandparents. You got to see your mum sometimes.

And so what if your parents weren't married? Mine were, and it doesn't seem to do them (or me) much good.

Matt

The doorbell rings. I stand at my window, and listen to Dave talking to someone at the front door. "It's a bit late for visiting," he says.

I stare at Mum's Uluru painting. "I need to find you," I say out loud.

"Find who?" Troy appears in my bedroom doorway. He walks in, usual wide grin stretched across his freckled face.

"Sorry about before." I say.

"No worries. It's forgotten." Troy picks up Mum's card. "Hey, cool picture. Who's it from?"

I feel myself tense. My arm flexes, itches to grab the card back from him. Then I realise it's the easiest way, the only way I'll be able to tell him about why my life is so messed up. I sit on the bed and watch his face while he reads.

"Holy crap! I thought your mum was dead."

"Me too."

"So that's why you've been wacko the last couple of days." He passes the card back and mumbles, "I don't know what to say."

Even though I'm pretty wound up, a grin slips out. "That'd be a first."

Troy pretends to look offended. "Have you told your dad about this? Is that why we didn't get into too much strife about the tank?"

"Na, that was some deal he did with the PC."

"So, what did he say about the card?"

The anger boils inside me again. "Haven't told him yet. Why should I? He's kept her from me for the last ten years."

"It must have been a hell of a shock."

"Yeah, it was."

"Why didn't you tell me?"

I lie back on the bed, feeling defeated. "I've been trying to process it. Why can't I have a normal life like yours?"

Troy laughs. "You think I'm normal?"

"Well, maybe not, but your family is. You have a mum and dad who are really into each other. And you've got a sister and grandparents – the whole 'happy family' thing."

Troy gives an exaggerated yawn. "Might seem ideal, but they're about as exciting as one of your dad's self-help books. *Nothing* ever happens in our house – not unless I make it."

I sit up and lean against the wall. "At least your parents don't lie to you."

Troy picks up a rubber and sharpener off my desk and starts juggling them. "So what are you going to do now?"

"Don't know." My voice is croaky. "She hasn't tried to contact me for the last ten years."

Troy stops juggling. "She must have her reasons. You should talk to her and find out what they are."

Pulling the Mayberry Girls' Grammar pin out of my drawer, I scratch the timber with it. "I dunno."

"She sent you the card. Maybe she wants to get to know you."

"You think?"

"Yeah, 'course." Troy starts pacing the room. "This is unbelievable. The only thing that goes missing in our house is my socks. We don't lose family members."

I stab the front of the drawer with the Mayberry pin. "Hilarious Troy – not."

"Sorry man, but this sort of stuff never happens to me. If you go looking for her, you can count me in."

I hand Troy the email from Scott Reesborough, and tell him what Scott told me on the phone. "I'm thinking of checking out this Barry Hill place. What do you reckon?"

Troy nods. "Sounds like a plan."

"Scott reckons she had some sort of a breakdown after Year Twelve. You don't think she's a nutter, do you?"

Troy looks at me as if I'm the one that's crazy. "I'd have a breakdown too if my parents made me do Year Twelve. We can head out to Barry Hill tomorrow, if you want."

"Thanks. But I'll be fine."

"Come off it. This is the most action I've had all year. You can't shut me out now."

"Yeah, well too bad. This is something I have to do by

myself."

Troy shrugs. "Suit yourself. But I want to know *everything* when you get back."

———————————————

Hey Leonardo,

I'm pretty freaked at the idea of seeing my mum after all this time. What if she never recovered from her breakdown?

No, she must have. She married Dave and had me, so she must have got better.

Is finding your long-lost mother a good idea or not?

Did it work for you?

Dumb I know, asking you all these questions. But I reckon you've got as much chance of giving me the answers as anyone else. And at least you won't lie.

Doesn't say much, does it?

Matt

Chapter Six

*If your son refuses to talk to you about a problem, act
as if nothing's wrong. Don't try and force the issue.*
Sons and the Single Parent –
Rosenbaum Tactic Number 23

Act as if nothing's wrong. That's Dave's plan for today. At breakfast, he says nothing about PC Huggins, the water tank, *Dave Hudson is a liar* or the ransacked bedroom that we never discussed either.

"Have a good day at school," Dave says cheerily as he saunters out the door.

I don't look up from the breadcrumb maze I'm making on my plate. I am not going to school. Why should I? Why should I do *anything* Dave wants me to do? Besides, school and listening to Mrs D and her sarcasm is a waste of time – a waste of minutes and hours I could make much better use of.

I'm the only one who gets off the bus at Barry Hill. The car park's empty. It's not like a normal hospital where kids and parents spill out of cars clutching cellophane-wrapped flowers..

There's a boy in a blue shirt with a red baseball cap on backwards, dragging a billycart to the top of a concrete path that leads to the car park. He pushes off and disappears down the hill.

I walk slowly towards the hospital. The grass needs a good mow, like the lawn at home. That's what happens when you only have one parent, and they work practically seven days a week. I offered to do the mowing once, but Dave said, "The lawnmower's too temperamental. If you don't know its habits, it's likely to take your leg off."

"Whatever." It wasn't like I was desperate to mow the lawn – I never asked again.

A red stone path winds up to Barry Hill. The main hospital

wing is two storeys high with an attic at the top. *Wonder who they keep up there!* This place sure has a weird vibe.

As I climb higher, the sun comes out, throws my shadow onto the concrete. Huge steps lead to double wooden doors covered in cobwebs. The shell of a centipede hangs upside down from one thread. I shiver. Maybe I should have let Troy come after all.

I try to open the massive dungeon-like doors. They're locked and won't budge. Is Mum in there? How can you seriously expect anyone to get well in a depressing place like this?

Hey Leonardo,

Seems like the mystery of Mum could be like the truth behind your Mona Lisa – impossible to discover.

Went to Barry Hill and it was closed. I don't mean "door shut, come back tomorrow" kind of closed. I mean gone. There is no Barry Hill "psychiatric facility" anymore.

Hasn't been any patients there for eight years.

So, when it comes to finding Mum, I'm back where I started, which is nowhere!

Where do I go from here? Who knows? Everyone has a theory on what's behind Mona Lisa's smile. That's what I need, a theory on how to find lost mothers who you thought were dead!

Your Lisa's not the only one who's an enigma.

Wish me luck, Leo.

Matt

I spend the rest of the day eating chocolate ice-cream, doodling on scrap paper sketchpads and making lists:

Why find Mum?
- She's my mother.
- Need to know why she left me.
- Need to know if she still wants to be my mother.
- Need to know where I come from.
- Need to know why Dave lied.
- Need my mother in my life.
- Need to know if she still loves me.

Where to look for her
- Psych hospital (Been there, didn't enjoy that!)
- Old school friends
- Relatives (like Aunt Alexa)
- Last resort – Dave!

Possible outcomes of finding her
- She won't want to know me.
- She will want to know me.
- She comes to live with me and Dave.
- I go and live with her.

Conclusion: I'll go crazy if I don't find out the truth.

I eat more ice-cream and think about what to do next.

Troy races in after school, backpack flung over his shoulder.

"What's she like?" he asks.

"Dunno, never saw her."

"Well, that's good isn't it? Maybe she recovered?'

My voice is flat, empty like Barry Hill. "She wasn't there. Nobody was. Place is closed down."

"What?"

"Nobody lives there any more."

Troy laughs. "You're kidding."

"No." I drop the spoon and it clangs into the empty ice-cream bowl.

"So, what will you do now?" Troy slaps his backpack at my feet.

"Dunno."

"There must be some other way to find her."

"Maybe. Mum had a sister, you know? My aunt Alexa."

"Why don't you just ring her?"

"Can't! I don't even know her last name, even though she's my aunt. She just sort of disappeared out of my life after we moved. I get a birthday card every year and that's about it."

Troy frowns. He picks up Mum's card. "Maybe you can find your mum through her art."

"How?" Uluru jumps out of the thin gold border – so real you can almost touch it. I wonder what it was like for Mum, living with someone like Dave who thinks that painting is something you do to your house when you want to sell it. Is that why Mum left him/us, because Dave was aesthetically challenged?

"You have to talk to your dad," says Troy. "He must know something."

I tap my foot on the leg of the coffee table. "Why should I trust him to be honest with me *this time*? I kick harder.

The table almost tips, and Troy catches it. "Tell him the truth – that you know your mum's not dead."

"I dunno."

Troy places the table firmly back where it was. "It's the only way. Want me to stick around while you do it?"

"No thanks, this is between me and Dave." I clench my fist. And unclench it. The anger's still there.

"Let us know how it goes." Troy picks up his pack and strolls out the door.

I'm still not sure this is the right thing to do. But now that I've made the decision, I wish Dave would hurry up and get home. I've hardly spoken to him for the last few days. He'll be so rapt that I'm actually talking to him again.

Until he finds out what I have to say.

Chapter Seven

I'm waiting at the kitchen table when Dave walks in the door. "Hey Matt!" He grabs the milk from the fridge and sits across from me. We don't really look at each other. We're like two people posed to look a certain way – to give a certain impression. Father and son carefully arranged to appear as if everything's good between them.

It makes me think of the way the angels look at each other in Leonardo's *Baptism of Christ*. Art is so important to me. And that's only one of the things that makes me different to lying Dave. I slouch in my chair, trying to fit my legs in the space between the seat and the floor.

Dave's hands are joined in front of him, resting on the table. "So how was your day?" He has on his "probing father" look – the one where he tries to see the inner workings of my brain.

How can he act as if nothing happened between us? As if I haven't been ignoring him for the last few days?

"How was yours." I shrug. My plan is to play his "patient listener" game – probe back at *him* till he admits the truth.

"Awesome."

That just makes me angry. "Mine was actually crap." I can't hold it any longer. I blurt out. "I know Mum's not dead!" There, how does that bombshell grab you?

It grabs him alright. His face goes rigid – fragile and stiff like clay slurry after it dries. Is he going to pretend he didn't hear me? He twitches in his seat, and blinks. I read a body language article once that said people who blink when they're talking to you aren't telling the truth.

I look him right in the eye. The anger keeps me cold. "No more lies, Dave. Don't say anything, if you're not going to tell me the truth."

"Uh ..."

"I need the truth."

Suddenly, he slumps over the table and starts to cry. He's crying! Dave *never* cries. His "Honest Dave" face crumples red.

"Smiling Dave" cries loud, gulping sobs.

I've never seen Dave – Dad – cry. It melts a sliver of ice inside me. I want to tell him not to be upset, to forget I said anything. But I can't let it go. I don't trust myself to speak because I don't know what to say.

Then anger overwhelms me again. It could be another tactic, Dave's way of avoiding the whole issue. Is this his way to avoid telling me the truth? I don't know what's real anymore. "Can't you be straight with me for once?" I fling back my chair and storm off. *I'm* crying now, red-hot anger pouring out of me like volcanic perspiration.

"Matt, wait!"

He stops me in the doorway.

"Why? So you can tell me more lies?"

"We need to talk."

I go back to my chair, but not to sit down again. I stand over him so he can feel as small as I felt when I discovered the truth. "Bit overdue, don't you think?"

He nods. "I don't blame you for being angry, Matt. Every day I've had to keep this from you. Every day it has sickened me. But I had no choice."

I snort. "Had no choice! You're always saying, 'We make our own choices in life'. Isn't that what Rosenbaum says? That's what you're always telling me anyway."

Dave's face is pale, his eyes unusually bright. His voice is soft, broken. "You were little. It was for your own good. I had to protect you."

"From what? My own mother! What was she, an axe murderer?"

"No, but–"

"So, why did I need protecting?"

"You were just a small child–"

"Yeah, well, in case you didn't realise, I haven't been a small child for years. What did she do that was so bad?"

He sighs. "Sit down, Matt. We need to talk this through."

"I'd rather stand."

"Fair enough."

I want this don't I? I confronted him with it. I clutch my stomach, hit by the urge to throw up. Can I handle the truth? What if my mother doesn't want me? What if she never wanted me?

I make it to the toilet just in time; kneel over the bowl and heave my guts out.

Dave follows and stands watching. "Are you okay?" His voice is almost back to normal

"What do you reckon?"

The door squeaks as he leans against it. "We can do this another time, Matt."

"No." More vomit rises inside me.

"I have something to show you. It's in the office safe." Dave jiggles his car keys nervously. "I'll be back in about half an hour. We'll talk then, okay?"

I nod. The front door slams and the car starts. What's so important that he keeps it in the office safe? What's so important, he never wanted me to know about it?

Hey Leonardo,

My life is layers of paint. Things keep getting peeled back and it's hard to know what's going to be revealed next.

Lies, lies and more lies?

Not sure where this journey's going to end but I have a bad feeling about what happens next.

Still, you and me, Leo, we have to know the truth, it's who we are.

Not sure Mrs D is going to get this letter either.

Matt

Chapter Eight

Dave walks into my room, carrying a black folder under his arm. "You think this is my fault, don't you?" he says.

"Isn't it?"

"Maybe. You figure it out."

Dave drops the folder on the bed in front of me and leaves. Inside is a newspaper article from the *Denyer Times*. I vaguely remember living in a place called Denyer before we moved here.

It's a front-page story with a photo of me, aged about five. I've seen one just like it in Dave's photo album, the one that doesn't have pictures of Mum.

A huge headline screams, *Mother Abandons Son in Shopping Centre.* It can't be true, can it?

> *A 28-year-old woman was taken into custody today after abandoning her son in the Denyer Shopping Centre. A witness said she saw the woman leave her young boy on a wooden seat and walk off. "I thought she was just going to look in a shop window," said jeweller Marg Johnson. "I was on my own and couldn't leave my store. Some customers came in and I got distracted. After they'd left, I looked out and saw that poor little boy still sitting there. No sign of the mother.*

I start to sweat. Memories and pictures rush through my head like a high-speed slide projector showing snapshots of my life.

I'm a little kid again, watching Mum walk away. I'm not afraid at first. But then she doesn't come back. A big lady with blond hair takes me into her shop. She offers me a lolly, but I don't want it. I want Mummy.

I want to stop reading but I can't.

> *Police sources say the woman has been charged and*

will undergo psychological evaluation pending her trial.
The boy's father was too distraught to comment.

Suddenly, I remember things about Mum: the invisible perfume aura that floated around her. When I was little that sweet smell made my tongue tingle.

I loved the way she smelled, and her softness when she cuddled me on her lap.

That day she took me into so many shops, buying me things I didn't even ask for. We went to a shoe shop. I tried on blue runners and she bought six pairs. The shop assistant packed them into little yellow cardboard boxes and put them into bags. There were too many to carry so we left a box at the shop.

Mum bought me chocolate ice-cream – lots of it. I felt sick.

"Sit down and rest while I look in some shops."

I was happy sitting on the seat but she never came back. Dave picked me up from the police station. He'd been running. When he hugged me his face was wet against mine.

I turn the pages. The more I read, the more I remember.

Mother Has a History of Abandonment ... Mrs Pearson, a neighbour of the accused, stated in court that this isn't the first time the boy has been left. "Six months ago, I heard crying next door. The front door was locked. I broke in through the side window. That poor little boy was all alone, crying for his mummy. I had to call the father home from work. That woman didn't turn up till two days later."

I remember; I remember falling asleep on the couch and waking up. I walked through the house looking for Mum, but she wasn't there. I remember Mrs Pearson cuddling me till Dad came home.

Senior Constable Smithers, a police officer involved in the shopping centre case said, "The mother was cautioned when the boy was just two years old for leaving him in a locked car outside a supermarket. She has a history of this type of behaviour and it seems to be escalating."

The last article shows Mum crying on the steps of the courthouse. There's a paragraph underneath the picture.

After a psychological evaluation of the mental state of the accused, Dave Hudson has been awarded full custody of his only son. The boy's mother, Zora Hudson has been granted supervised access.

Psychological evaluation? Mental state? Supervised access? What does all that mean? There's nothing in any of the papers to say what happened to Mum after that.

It must have been after the court case that Dave told me Mum had died that day at the shopping centre. That was the last time I saw her.

Lying on my bed, I watch a spider crawling across the ceiling.

Dave walks in and sits next to me. "Are you okay?"

I can't stop shaking. Guess it must be shock – the teachers talked to us about that in Phys Ed.

"Are you okay, Matt?"

The words creep out of my mouth. They sound small, like a little kid. "Think so. I remember things."

Dave puts his hand on my shoulder. "It wasn't your fault, you know."

"No?"

"She couldn't cope. She always loved you. She just couldn't handle life."

"Don't think I can either, right now."

"Don't be hard on yourself, Matt. This is a lot to deal with."

You're telling me?

Dave puts a hand on my shoulder. "I understand about the water tank now. What you did wasn't right, but I understand why you did it."

I shrug his hand away. "Yeah! Well, I still don't understand what *you* did. She was *my* mother!"

"I'm sorry I lied to you, Matt. I really thought it was best."

The problem is, Dave, you just kept lying. I turn away from him and put my hands over my ears.

Dave leaves behind the black folder that tells me so much, but hardly answers anything.

Mum left me in a shopping centre on my own. I was just a kid. Anything could have happened to me. Why would she do that? Was I such a bad kid?

What about the psychological evaluation? Is she mad?

My head pounds. A thick haze of memories spin around in my head. Fear thumps in my chest.

Hey Leonardo,

Troy got me a book from the library, Leonardo da Vinci: the Complete Paintings.

It would be so amazing to paint with another artist, like that picture you did with Verrocchio – the one of Tobias.

Love that pic. Good, but bad too. I feel like that fish you painted with the googly eyes, hanging by a painful thread, no escape. Is that how you felt when you painted it? Were you trapped? Tied to Verrocchio? Did you want to break away, do your own thing? Your dog in that picture looks like it was added in later. Painting in layers lets you hide things – mistakes.

What does each layer of paint really tell us about you? I wish I could talk to you, Leo. Really know you. You were such a genius. Maybe you could help me sort out the mess in my head.

Matt

Chapter Nine

Grabbing three new spray cans from the garage, I head to Troy's house. His Mum answers the door. "You okay, Matt?"

Troy must have told her. I nod. It makes the pounding in my head worse.

"You can talk to me anytime."

"Thanks."

Troy's mum's a counsellor. She spends all day listening to people with 'issues'. Don't reckon she really wants to add me to the list. She's being polite, like Dave when he tells people they have a really nice house, even though it's an absolute dump. My stomach clenches. I don't want to think about Dave right now.

"Troy, Matt's here."

She seems not to notice the spray cans in my hand. But Troy does. "Art therapy?" he asks.

His mother does not need to know my plans. "Come on." I lope off down the street.

At the water tank, we flop down on the grass. "You told your dad?"

"Yep."

"And."

I tell Troy about Mum dumping me at the shops – and all the other dumpings – some I don't remember at all. "Don't reckon she ever wanted me."

"You don't know that!" Troy stares at me intently, more serious than I've ever seen him, like he needs me to believe what he's saying. "You don't know what was going on with her at the time."

Dave and his pathetic apology sucks. But what hurts the most – Mum and me. What makes a mother dump her kid? How could she think that was the best choice she could make?

I feel like that piece of eggshell that falls into the cup when you crack the egg. It floats around on the top without a purpose and yet it's stuck there, helpless to change anything.

Troy reaches for a can. "I'm happy to help."

Scuffing at the ground in front of the tank, I flick fine dust into the side. "You know what PC Huggins said would happen if we do this tank again," I warn him.

Troy shrugs. "We'll smell that garlic coming a mile off. Have plenty of time to get away. And in any case, what's the big deal? It's not as if we're doing any damage. We're beautifying the place."

"Eco art," I say.

Troy takes the west side of the tank and I take the east, the one where the sun comes up.

Once I have the spray can in my hand, all I want to do is paint. I take Mum's card from my pocket and rest it against the tank. The sun starts to go down. I have to move fast. I spray huge sweeping arcs in deep ochre, and etch details using a darker can, with a fine nozzle. I stand back to look. Not bad, but it doesn't have the texture of Mum's picture. You can get brightness with spray cans, but not details, not the blending of colours that you get with a brush.

The sky's the hardest, getting the colour right, the shading, so that when you look at it from different angles, the picture changes – kind of like a hologram.

Troy finishes his art. He's into sci-fi, and he paints an eagle with robot feet instead of talons. It's cool.

We're sort of like Leonardo and Verrocchio painting together, only working on separate pieces.

Troy stands back to look at my side of the tank. "Wow! That's awesome," he says. "Your mum's not the only one with talent."

"Wonder what else I got from her," I mumble. "Those newspaper pieces said she was wacko."

"Everyone's a bit wacko – even me." Troy points a spray can at me and presses the nozzle. I duck and run off around the tank with him chasing me.

We collapse in front of the eagle robot, the almost empty spray cans at our feet.

"I look more like Mum. I'm nothing like Dave really, am I? I'm brown, he's blond. My eyes are brown, his are blue."

"Does your Mum have a face like a cane toad too?"

I pick up a handful of dust and toss it at Troy. "Very funny."

Troy flicks back his curly hair. "I'm glad I don't look like my olds."

"Can you be serious?"

"Sorry, I'll try." Troy pokes out his tongue until it covers his top lip, and makes it looks like he has a clown mouth.

I try not to look at him. "Do you reckon I could be crazy like her? You'd have to be crazy, wouldn't you, to leave a little kid alone in a car, and a house, and a shopping centre."

Troy jabs me in the ribs. "You're mad, sometimes," he says. "But you're not crazy."

I wish for once he'd stop fooling around. I grab my cans and stand up. "This isn't a joke, man. This is my life."

Troy gets to his feet too. "I know, but you have to chill. You can't help stuff that happened to you when you were a kid. And you can't sort things out when you're all worked up."

"Give me a break. Have you been reading Rosenbaum too?" I fight the urge to chuck a can at him.

Troy won't let it go. "Maybe you could talk to your mum, ask her why she did it."

I know he's right but the problem is, I have to find her first.

I wag school again and spend the day going over my "Mum" lists, trying to think where she might be.

- In another town?
- In another state?
- In another country?

How did people find each other before the Internet? I try an Australian search then a World search for Mum, but there's nothing. It's like Zara Templeton or Hudson or whatever she calls herself never existed. But she did. She's my mother. I try other search engines, but still nothing! I yell my frustration. Punch the wall. But none of it helps. I need a break.

I need a loud action movie that I can crank up to full volume. I'm flicking through sites on my tablet when Dave strolls in from work, and sits down next to me, uninvited. Doesn't even ask me to turn the volume down. Rosenbaum must have got him onto the next phase. "Try and be understanding."

Dave sighs. "I'll tell you anything you want to know."

How can I trust him? How do I forget that he *lied* to me, pretend it never happened, forgive him for "protecting me" from my *own* mother. What a load of bull! She might have been a bit crazy back then, but she's probably fine now, and I'm old enough to look after myself. Some kids leave home at fifteen.

I stop searching. "Anything? You'll answer any questions?"

He nods.

"How will I know you're telling me the truth?"

"You're going to have to start trusting me again some time." Dave gets up and goes to the kitchen.

I'm still looking for the perfect movie when Dave yells, "Tea's ready". Just as the doorbell rings.

When Dave opens the door, a blast of garlic bursts into the house followed by PC Huggins who shakes his finger at me like I'm about ten. "I'm not going to take things so lightly on you this time, Matt Hudson."

At the table I wind noodles around my fork.

"You've been at the water tank again haven't you, young vandal?"

"Steady on," says Dave. "You don't know it was him."

The PC folds his arms across his large chest. "You going to deny it?"

"No."

"Yeah, well last time you got away with it, but not this time."

Dave moves in front of me as if he's trying to be my shield. "Ease up, Clem, he's just a kid."

The PC laughs. He sounds like a camel with hiccups. "Just a kid? He's bigger than you, Dave, and old enough to know better."

"He's having his tea, Clem. Can you give it a rest?"

The PC scowls at me. "He's going to be charged."

Dave takes a deep breath. The muscle twitches under his left eye, but his voice is calm. "At least let me talk to Matt first. Get to the bottom of it."

The PC looks at his watch, then pats his stomach.

Dave gently guides him to the front door. "You go home and eat. I'll bring Matt down to the station after work tomorrow. Is that okay? We'll sort it out then."

I don't think the PC is all that happy, but everyone in town likes "Honest Dave", so he lets us get away with it, for the time being.

His parting words are: "It's vandalism, Dave! Charges will be laid this time."

Dave nods as he shuts the front door. "Yeah, rightio, Clem. Like I said, we'll sort this out tomorrow."

After the PC leaves, Dave sits next to me and eats as if nothing happened. I can't believe he's so calm. He has definitely been consulting Rosenbaum. I wonder if there's a chapter in *Sons and the Single Parent* on how to help your kid deal with the fact that you've lied to him for the last ten years.

While we wash the dishes, Dave says, "We'll talk about the water tank tomorrow. After we've both had a good night's sleep."

I shrug. "Whatever."

Hey Leonardo,

Painting huge is such an adrenaline rush, isn't it? Did you find it hard to go back to the small stuff? Maybe that's why you went on to your inventing, and sculpture?

I'm not sorry I did the water tank. Just hope Troy doesn't cop it.

If you have talent, why hide it?

Matt

Chapter Ten

I'm totally blown away to see a photo of my painting on the front page of the local paper with the headline: *Welcome facelift for old water tank.*

Unreal! *Welcome facelift?* Someone actually likes my art. Down at the bottom of the page there's a phone poll so you can ring in and say what you think of it.

On page three, there's a photo of the mayor standing next to the pic that Troy painted. According to the paper, the mayor wants to know who the artists were and he says he "can't see any reason why the murals can't stay".

Just before I head off to school, I get a phone call from Steve Bridges – he recognised my work.

"Congratulations on your awesome artwork, Matt," he says.

"Thanks."

"Have you thought any more about my classes?"

"Yeah."

"If money's an issue," he says. "We can deal with that."

"It's not the money. It's Dave. He doesn't like me painting."

Up until now, I always wondered why he was so negative about my art. Now I know that it's because of Mum. It's because she paints. He's scared too, scared I'll turn out like her. I bet that it's it. I have to find out if I'm right. "Gotta go, Steve."

"Fair enough. I'll talk to your dad myself. See if I can change his mind."

Fat chance! "Thanks. That would be great."

At school Troy has already told anyone who will listen that he and I were the ones that painted the water tank.

First period is History. "Interesting artwork, boys," says Mrs D.

Troy stands and bows, and tries to drag me up with him, but I stay in my seat. Everyone laughs.

Mrs D focuses on me. "Perhaps if you applied the same dedication and creativity to your History assignment, Mr Hudson, you might make more progress."

I nod. Whatever.

All day Troy makes the most of the celebrity status – tells Tina that we're going to be famous artists one day. She just rolls her eyes and walks off. I spend most of the time thinking about Mum. Wish she could see my painting. Wonder if she'd think I was any good.

After school Troy and I sit at my kitchen table chomping on cheese sandwiches with bread. That's what Dave always calls them. He always whinges because I cut the cheese so thick.

"What are you going to do about your mum?" Troy's teeth are yellow with cheddar.

"Maybe I should just forget the whole thing. There must be a reason she stayed away till now."

Troy cuts another slab of cheese. "It probably took her all this time to find you."

"Can't have looked too hard."

Troy sticks the cheese on bread and slaps another slice on top. "Maybe she wasn't allowed to see you. Didn't she go to court after that business in the shopping centre?"

I kick the leg of the chair on the other side of the table. "She was allowed supervised access, just chose not to do it. What if I find her and she doesn't even like me?"

Troy laughs. "As if that's likely. All mothers have to like their kids. It's an unwritten law."

"Wait here." I go to my room and get the black folder Dave gave me. I shove it in front of Troy. "Read this – then try telling me that she liked me."

Troy's voice interrupts my thoughts of Mum. "And you haven't seen her since the shopping centre?"

I wipe a wet patch from under my eye, and shake my head, not trusting myself to speak yet.

"Why don't you Google her?" says Troy.

"I have. Couldn't find anything."

"Not even about the court case?"

"Nuh!"

"That's weird!" Troy keeps looking through the short history of my life in newsprint.

He turns to me. "Did you even read these?"

What's he on about? "Course I did."

"And what was the name you Googled?"

"Zara Templeton. That was the name in the bible."

"Yeah, well I don't think that's what she's called."

"What are you talking about?"

Troy points to the article about the court case where Dave got custody of me. "Her name's Zora, not Zara. See!"

I go back to my room. Troy follows. I fling open my desk drawer and rummage through until I find the bible. I open it to the first place. Troy could be right. I read it as an "A", but it could be an "O". "I thought it was just a typo in the paper. "How come Kathryn Armain and Scott Reesborough never said anything?"

"They probably just thought you couldn't spell."

"You're so funny, Troy."

Troy bows. "I try to be."

It's not right, not even knowing your own mother's name. I key in Zora Hudson, and am just about to click on "search" when Dave walks in.

"Good news, boys." Dave glances at the screen and raises an eyebrow.

"Really?" I say in a pretend-bright voice.

"You're not going to be charged for painting the water tank."

That's the good news?

"They should be paying us," says Troy.

I agree.

"You think?" Dave rolls his eyes.

Swivelling my chair around to look at him, I lean back with my hands behind my head, trying my best to hide what's displayed on the computer.

"So, what happened?"

"The councillors took a vote and decided it makes the old water tank look better than it has in years."

"Cool. I'd better let my olds know. Catch you, Matt. See you, Mr H."

After Troy leaves, Dave moves closer to my computer and I can't stop him from seeing what's on the screen.

"What are you doing, Matt?" he says quietly.

I keep my voice firm. "Trying to find Mum."

Dave sits on my bed. "You're asking for trouble, Matt. She'll only bring you grief."

"Being without her has brought me plenty of that already."

He runs the edges of the quilt through his fingers. "I'm sorry I lied to you, but it was for your own good."

"You keep saying that."

"That's because it's true. I know what she's like, what she's capable of. Don't forget I was married to her for a long time."

"Exactly! You were *married* to her. I'm her kid. It's different. We're blood."

Dave strides out of the room. Is he mad with me? Good.

I press "search" on Zora Hudson. All that comes up are archive references for articles about the court case. Don't need to read any more of them. I check out Zora Templeton. Only one hit, a piece about an art comp Mum won when she was seventeen. But that's it. It's like she really did die. Like she ceased to exist after the court case.

Dave comes back with a thick photo album. He lays it on the bed next to me. Okay, so that's why he disappeared. "Where was that?"

Dave smiles. "You don't know *all* my secrets. I've been keeping this under the bed. I guess I always knew you'd want to know about her one day. I was just hoping it wouldn't happen till you were an adult and she couldn't manipulate you."

The anger comes pouring out of me. "Can't you give her a break?"

Dave's voice is calm and Rosenbaumish. "You don't know her, Matt."

Just for once I want him to show me what he's really feeling.

I fling the black folder of newspaper clippings at his feet. "I don't care that the judge wouldn't let her have shared custody? That doesn't prove anything. The judge was probably just trying to punish her because mothers aren't supposed to leave their kids. Lots of fathers walk out on mothers, but people seem to think that's okay." How would a judge know if she loved me or not?

Dave hesitates. "She left you more than once, Matt."

"I know that. It was ages ago anyway."

"People don't change."

"How do you know?"

The photo album is closed on his lap. He gestures to the place next to him. "Come and sit with me. Let me tell you about her."

Maybe he's finally ready to tell me the truth.

On the first page is a photo of Mum and Dad standing outside some university. I can't read the name of it because it has been cut off in the picture. Mum doesn't look much older than me.

"You went to uni together?"

Dave nods. "That's how we met. I was in the last year of my sound engineering course, and she was studying art."

"You were a sound engineer?" That's freaky. I thought Dave had been born a real estate agent.

Dave seems distracted. As if he's looking back. "Yeah. I was good too."

"How come you stopped?"

Dave turns the next page to a photo of him and Mum at a twenty-first birthday party. "She was gorgeous, your mother, when I first met her. Bright, funny, always smiling."

"What changed?"

"That was only half of who she was."

I don't get it. I look at Dave for answers.

"That's who she was when she was 'up'. Other times she wouldn't talk, locked herself in a room and refused to come out. Or she cried and cried, and I couldn't do anything to make her happy."

Dave turns the page to a photo of him and Mum in the park. She's pushing my pram and Dave has a huge basset hound on a red lead. He grins. "That was Romulus. Great mutt."

It's like I don't even know this man. He never let *me* have a dog.

"Things were good with us at the start. Till she stopped taking her medication. Said she couldn't paint when she was on it. That's when she started to do really unpredictable things ..."

"Like leave me alone in cars?"

Dave nods. "It was an illness, something she was born with, a chemical imbalance in her brain. She couldn't help it, you know."

"Couldn't you make her take her tablets?"

Dave's mouth tenses into a hard line. "Nobody can make your mother do anything she doesn't want to do."

"You gave up your job?"

"I had to work away from home a lot. Your mother got worse and worse. Started doing more and more bizarre things like that time she left you at home on your own while she went to see a movie and go shopping. You were just a little kid. It got to the stage I didn't feel safe leaving you with her for long."

"That's why you got a job in real estate?"

Dave flicks to the next page. "It was long hours, but at least I was home every night to make sure you were safely tucked in bed. And at least it meant I wasn't far away when she left you in that shopping centre."

A cold shiver goes down my spine, and I don't exactly know why. Is it a past memory or a fear of what's ahead?

Hey Leonardo,

Life is like a painting. Every time you look at it from another angle you see something different.

It's not about colour or shading or even composition. It's all about perspective – and mood – and looking under the surface.

Matt

Chapter Eleven

Dave wants to help me look for Mum. He's not happy about it, but he says that if I'm determined to find her, he wants to be with me when I do. I'm not sure I want him there, but right now I'll take all the help I can get.

Aunt Alexa, Mum's sister is our next lead, but Dave hasn't seen her since the court case.

Dave moves towards his bedroom, his phone in his hand. "I'll ring her and let you know what happens," he says.

"No way." I'm not quite ready to trust him yet. "If you're going to ring her, it has to be on speaker so I can hear every word ..."

"Not sure that's such a good idea."

"You promised you'd help me. You promised no more hiding stuff."

Dave nods. I flop down at the kitchen table while he keys in the number and puts the phone on.

"Hi, Alexa, it's Dave Hudson."

"Dave?"

"Yeah."

"It's been a while."

Dave turns up all the coffee mugs drying on the sink. "Yes it has."

"Did ... did ... Matt get my birthday card?"

"He did." Dave paces next to the table.

"Is ... everything okay?"

Dave stops abruptly and fires out the words. "Matt got a birthday card from Zora."

Thump! Sounds like she dropped the phone.

I take a deep breath.

Dave waits. "Are you there, Alexa?"

For a moment there's silence on the other end of the phone.

"Yes ..." She sounds as if she's crying.

Dave glares at me. "Alexa, are you...okay?"

A sniffle comes through the speaker. "I'm ... a bit ... surprised, that's all ..."

"Us, too," Dave's whispers.

Dave and I look at each other awkwardly, waiting for Aunt Alexa to stop crying.

"How's ... Matty ... taking it?"

Dave sighs. "About as well as can be expected."

"Poor kid ... must have been a shock."

It was, and I'm not a kid.

Dave's voice is firmer. "He wants to find his mother."

Aunt Alexa seems to recover a bit. "I don't know where she is. Haven't seen her for about five years. Not since she was last in psychiatric care."

"At Barry Hill?" That muscle in the corner of Dave's eye twitches like crazy.

"No, they closed that place down years ago."

Thanks for telling me.

Dave starts pacing again. "So, what happened?"

Aunt Alexa's voice goes soft and shaky. "She had a bad episode. Spent three months in Gardenvale Hospital Acute Psychiatric Unit."

Dave sits on the table next to me. "Then where did she go?"

"To a hostel for a while. When she came out she said she wanted a new start."

"How many times have I heard that?" says Dave.

Aunt Alexa is crying again. "She didn't want anything to do with her old life, even her family. She moved away, changed her number and we haven't heard from her since."

Dave's breath is quick and shallow. "Is there anyone else who'd know where she is?"

"Can't think of anybody. If I do, I'll let you know."

That's it! End of conversation?

"Thanks, Alexa. Sorry to upset you."

Sorry to upset *her*. What about me?

Aunt Alexa sniffs. "I thought I'd moved on ... you know."

"Zora's not that easy to move on from."

"Give my love to Matty, won't you?"

"I will." Dave pushes the disconnect button.

"That was helpful – NOT!" Another dead end.

Dave's voice is still uneven. "I'm sorry, Matt. I tried. I don't know what else you expect me to do."

"Telling me the truth in the first place would have been a good start."

I slam the front door shut behind me.

At school I stew over Dave's call to Aunt Alexa. I hated the sadness in her voice. But I still wanted to yell into the speaker, "I'm not a kid anymore Aunt Alexa. I have the right to find her, she's my mother." And, "How come you butted out of my life just like everyone else?" I can't believe it. Mum's out there somewhere, but nobody, not even her own sister can tell me where she is.

I can't focus on anything Mrs D says, can't get comfortable. Why do they make school furniture for jockeys? I've seriously outgrown these tables. Without even stretching, I keep touching the chair of the person in front of me; Tina Armstrong, Class Goddess, Troy's crush. I pull my legs back under me.

Troy, on the other hand, is deliberately trying to attract her attention.

"She's looking hot today." He signals to me. He sticks out his foot and tries to hook it under the leg of Tina's chair.

Mrs D hears the scraping and peers over the top of her glasses at us. Troy stops moving, and Mrs D goes on talking. Troy sinks lower in his chair. He stretches his legs out too far and the chair slips back. He lands on the ground with a thump that Mrs D can't miss. She marches across the room, and looks down at him, sprawled on the floor.

"Troy Daly! What on earth are you doing down there?"

"It's Tina. I think I've fallen for her."

The rest of the class groans. Tina looks at Troy and asks, "Do you need a hand?"

"Yeah, thanks."

Tina steps out of her chair. She pauses for maximum impact,

then puts her hands together and starts a slow handclap. Most of the class joins in. Troy picks himself up, takes a bow and sits back down.

The whole thing's pretty funny, but I seriously need to be somewhere else.

"I reckon she fancies me," says Troy.

"Whatever."

"Mr Hudson and Mr Daly," interrupts Mrs D, "perhaps you'd like to let us get on with the History lesson and leave the social chat for lunchtime?"

"Not really," I mutter. I'm so sick of adults treating me like a little kid – as if what I think doesn't matter.

Mrs D walks between the lines of tables. She stands over me, hands on hips. "Then perhaps you'd like to get out of my class so I can teach those who want to learn."

"Fine with me." I pick up my books and leave.

Troy follows. Twenty-two pairs of eyes watch us leave.

Second time I've been thrown out of class in less than two weeks. I'm on a roll. "Let's hit the water tank."

I can't wait to get away from school and all the stuff that they think is important, but doesn't mean anything at all when you've just found out your dead mum is NOT DEAD!

It's warm – we sit in the shadow of the water tank and talk about Mum.

"I don't care what anybody says. I'm going to find her?" I pick up a stone and toss it into the distance, watch it being jolted about as it rolls down the hill on an uncontrolled path that seems to mirror my life. "She has to be somewhere."

"Dah!" Troy skids a stone off down the hill after mine. "Somebody has to know a painter with her talent," he says.

He's right. But who?

We wait till three-thirty then head to Troy's house. "No need for our olds to know we got kicked out of school," he says.

Troy goes straight to the fridge and drags out a chocolate

cake. Why can't Dave ever cook anything like that? We sit at the dining table munching cake and washing it down with huge glasses of milk. Angie, Troy's sister walks in with a group of giggling friends.

"Our basketball went over the fence," she says. "Could you get it for us, please, please?" She has Troy's freckled smile.

"Sure." Troy gets to his feet and Angie's friends look at him as if he's some kind of superhero.

When he comes back from his rescue mission, Troy shows me what he's done on his History assignment. He's up to about letter number six. And they're all really good, full of detail about his life and family. Not so easy for me. Half my family's missing and as far as the life bit goes, there's not much I want to share.

Troy's mum breezes in from work, wearing her never-ending smile. "Like something else to eat or drink, boys?"

I've just finished my second massive slice of chocolate cake. "No thanks, Mrs Daly. If I don't eat my tea, Dave's likely to go into a panic and think I've turned anorexic or something."

Troy's mum raises an eyebrow when I call my father by his first name, but she doesn't say anything.

"Thanks." Troy pushes his empty plate forward.

Mrs Daly slides another huge slab onto the plate and sits it in front of Troy. "Make sure you eat your tea too," she says and heads out the back door.

I trace my finger around the rim of my empty plate.

"You thinking about your mum?"

I nod. "Wonder what she's like now. If she's okay?"

These questions keep crashing around in my head. They won't leave me alone.

Hey Leonardo,

Your portraits are unreal. You get how people are with each other – every line and head tilt is always just right. The unspoken connections. Wonder if I'll ever be able to translate what I see, how I feel, into art.

I can block out everything when I look at your paintings. It's like getting transported to a whole different world – one where I can just watch and not have to get involved in what's going on.

The more I discover, Leo, the more I want to know about you and your work.

Think I'm becoming obsessed, at least that's what Troy reckons.

Matt

Chapter Twelve

Mrs D is boring and sarcastic but she does have her good side. I guess we all do. She organised an excursion, which is good for two reasons. One, we get out of class for a day. Two, it's to the museum and the art gallery.

"Why can't we go somewhere decent like Luna Park or Movie World?" asks Troy.

"Art gallery, Troy," I say. "We're going to the art gallery."

"Yeah, so?"

"Apart from the fact I thought you liked painting, Mum's an artist. Maybe I'll find out something about her."

Troy grins. "Good point."

On the bus, I'm in my own world, thinking about Mum when an apple hits me on the back.

"Wake up, Hudson," says a voice from the back seat. It's Skink. That guy's a pain. They call him Skink because he darts around everywhere and flicks his tongue as if he's catching flies. Thinks it's cool or something.

Bits of food and paper bags fly around in all directions. Mrs D yells, "That's enough!"

Nobody pays attention. The missiles keep coming. I duck and just miss copping an orange in the head. Troy has a Vegemite sandwich in his hand, ready to take aim, when the bus screeches to a halt. He's thrown against the seat in front, right into the back of Tina Armstrong. The sandwich ends up in her hair. She picks it out and tosses it back at Troy. "What do you think you're doing, bird brain? Leave me alone, will you?"

Aaron the bus driver, a man with axe-handle shoulders, storms up the aisle. Everyone stops, sits back down and hides their missiles behind their backs.

"I've had enough," he bellows. "Any more of this, I'll throw you all off the bus and you can walk back to school!"

The rest of the trip to the museum is just a hum of people talking in soft voices. Nobody dares leave their seats.

The most exciting exhibit is Phar Lap, the famous racehorse who died in America, although he doesn't look dead. Whoever recreated him must have been an artist. Phar Lap looks like he's about to leap off his pedestal and trot out of the museum.

"Isn't he awesome?" I nudge Troy.

"I dunno, he looks stuffed to me."

Tina Armstrong gives Troy another one of her scathing looks. Later, when Troy's at the toilets, she asks me, "Why do you hang around with that guy?"

"You have to get to know him. He's really cool. We've been best friends since we started school."

"Pity he hasn't grown up since then." Tina moves away as Troy comes back.

"Were you two talking about me?" he asks.

I shrug and Troy punches me on the shoulder. "She's got the hots for me, hasn't she? Yes! I knew she wouldn't be able to resist me."

I roll my eyes. "Yeah."

"Hey, look, she's heading off that way." Troy points towards the prehistoric exhibition. "Let's follow."

But before he can pester Tina again, Mrs D calls the class together and herds us back on the bus.

I can't wait to get to the gallery. Once we arrive we're not allowed off the bus until the driver has bellowed another warning. "Back here in two hours or I go without you."

We pile up the gallery steps and through the glass doors. "Australian exhibits, this way." Mrs D guides us to a large room full of the works by contemporary Australian artists. Each picture has a brass plate engraved with the name of the painting and its creator. Troy stops to look at an abstract painting by an artist who looks like he used to be a pasta chef. There are noodles of colour splashed together on the canvas; it doesn't look like anything real.

"Dunno what people see in this stuff," Troy says. "Reckon my little sister could do better."

I walk to the back of the room to look at one of the Archibald

Prize finalists. It's a portrait of a famous comedian, and it's pretty cool.

I turn to the painting on the opposite wall, a picture of Katherine Gorge. I recognise the colours, and the style. I let out a whoop. Mrs D turns around. Troy rushes over.

"Hey, check this out," I say.

It's an amazing painting. Massive cliffs either side reaching down to this trickle of water that seems insignificant. The colours are so real and so deep you can picture yourself there. There's a small brass plate next to the painting. *Deepest Fears* by Zorina.

Zora – short for Zorina? I'm sure it's her. Why isn't her last name on the plaque? Why is she making it so hard for me?

Troy stares at the painting. "Your mum?" he asks.

I nod. "Think so."

"Awesome." Troy looks around the room. "We should drag Tina over here. Do you reckon she'd be impressed?"

"No," I say. I don't want anyone to know that my mum did this.

"But it's so cool," Troy argues. "I thought you'd want people to know."

"No."

Part of me is proud that my mum created something so awesome. But what if she is crazy? What if everyone finds out I have a loony in the family?

"What will I say to Tina if she wants to meet her?" I ask Troy.

"I guess you're right. Still, I reckon it's pretty cool, having a famous mum."

"It would be even cooler if I knew where to find her."

"Maybe you could write to the gallery and tell them you're doing a school project on Zorina. They might have some info," says Troy.

"Good idea."

All the way home in the bus my mind is buzzing with thoughts about Mum and her paintings. I can hardly believe it.

My dead Mum is alive. And she's a well-known painter – sort of famous, in fact.

The minute I get home, I race upstairs, and email the gallery:

Dear Sir/Madam,

I loved 'Deepest Fears' by Zorina which I saw in your gallery.

I have decided to do a school assignment on this great artist and was wondering if you could tell me about her.

Does she live in Australia? How old is she? Does she still paint?

I would really appreciate any information you can give me for my project.

Thanks a lot.

Yours truly,

Matt Hudson

Finally, a week later, I get a reply – an envelope from the Gallery's Education Unit. I text Troy to tell him I have mail. He texts back: "B right there".

I can't wait that long. Fingers shaking, I rip the envelope open.

Don't know what I expected. I guess I was hoping for an address, phone number, home town, anything. But of course, it's never that easy.

All the envelope contains is a brief letter and a bio sheet on Zorina. It still doesn't mention her last name, doesn't give a lot of personal stuff about her, just her place of birth and the fact that she now lives in regional area.

"Regional area!" That really narrows it down – not!

Troy races in the door and I show him the pathetic "nothing" bio.

"Why don't we post something online?" he says. "We could

scan that photo you found in your dad's room and ask if anyone knows her or where she lives."

The photo is old and faded, but the scan doesn't come out too bad. We muck around on the computer for an hour, then we get a hit – several hits.

"I think I've found her! According to Katie57, she calls herself Zora Matthews now." Did she rename herself after me? Why start a new life without me, but use my name?

My eyes sting. Maybe what she said in the letter is true. Maybe she never did stop loving me. Either Dave lied again, or he never really knew her.

Who should I believe? The Dave who told me she was dead or the Dave who now reckons he wants to help me find her? Could I be more confused?

I search the Yellow Pages online for Mum's address. I find a listing in a place called Hillton. Can't be too many people around with the name Zora Matthews. Surely?

My hand shakes as I write down the telephone number for the person who could be my mother.

An online map shows that Hillton's only a couple of hours away by train. I can get there and back in a day while Dave's at work. He doesn't even have to know about it. He says he wants to help me, but I have to do this bit on my own. I have to give Mum a chance to tell her side of the story.

Hey Leonardo,

I'm getting close to finding Mum.

I feel like I'm your Tobias in Tobias and the Angel – on a journey with so many possible outcomes.

Wish me luck. (I hope I don't need it.)

Matt

PS – Dave has finally agreed to let me do Saturday art classes. I think Steve Bridges talked him into it. Troy thinks he might join too.

Thanks to Katie57 I have the ten-digit PIN to my mother. Get the numbers right and I can bring back the dead. It's too freaky. But I still have to find the guts to dial the code.

I'm petrified. She must have her reasons for staying away, just as Dave has his useless reasons for keeping us apart.

Troy grabs my mobile phone off the kitchen table and hands it me. "You've got your mum's number – now ring it," he says.

"What do I say to her? 'Hi, Zora. I'm your son.' Don't want to give her a heart attack."

"You won't. She's your mother."

"What if she doesn't want to know me?"

"She wants you to find her. She sent you that card, didn't she?"

I roll my eyes at him. "So, why didn't she include a return address?"

"Maybe she wants you to seek her out. That way she'll know she isn't forcing herself on you, that you really want to find her."

"But what if she changed her mind since she sent the card?"

Troy shakes his head. "Just ring her, will you? Put us all out of our misery."

"Easy for you to say."

"Do you want me to do it?" Troy tries to grab the phone from me.

"No, I will!" I swallow and dial the number. After three rings I hang up.

"What are you doing, Matt?"

"What if she's not there?"

"Then you ring back later."

Stomach churning, I dial the number again. It stops ringing, someone picks up. "Zora Matthews speaking."

It's her! I know her voice. I remember it. She's there on the other end of the phone – not dead. She's alive. My mother's alive!

Maybe I should leave the whole thing alone. I can't think of a single thing to say.

"Hello, is anybody there?" says my mother.

"Y-y-yes."

"Hello. Can I help you?"

Sounds like she's getting annoyed. What if she hangs up? I have to do something fast so I say the first thing that comes into my head. "It's me, M-M-Matt. I think you might be my mother." My stomach does somersaults. There's a long silence at the other end, but at least she doesn't hang up.

"What makes you think that?" She doesn't sound annoyed any more. And she didn't say I couldn't be her son.

"I'm Matt Hudson," I say. "Ten years ago my dad told me that my mother died. Her name was Zora, like yours."

Her voice floats back through the phone to me, soft and low, like a whisper of wind through the trees. "What can you tell me about your father?" She sounds scared too. It makes me braver.

"His name's Dave Hudson. He's forty-three and he's a real estate agent."

She doesn't say anything. I'm not sure what to do next.

"So what do you think?" I ask quickly, desperate to hear her voice again. It seems to take ages for her to talk.

Her words come out all choked up. "Why are you ringing me, Matt?" she asks.

"I got a birthday card. It was signed "Love, Mum". Did you send it?"

"Yes." Her voice is firmer, as if she's glad she did.

Troy taps me on the shoulder. "Is she your mother?" he hisses.

I give him the thumbs up, and say into the phone, "I need to talk to you. I need to know why you left."

For ages, there's silence and at first, I think she must have hung up.

"Come and see me, Matt. We'll talk. It's complicated."

That's a good sign. She wants to see me. "When?"

She hesitates. "Next weekend, if that's okay with your dad."

I suck in my breath. "I can make my own decisions."

"He's your father."

I can't believe she's taking his side. "I don't owe him anything. He lied. He told me you were dead."

"We'll talk about this when you come. There's a train to Hillton on Saturday morning. If you miss that one, you'll have to wait till Sunday."

"Don't worry, I won't miss it."

Mum laughs. "My house isn't far from the station." She gives me directions. "Look forward to seeing you on the weekend," she says.

I hang up the phone and flop back in my chair.

"So?" says Troy.

"I can't believe it. I'm going to see my mother."

Hey Leonardo,

I was flicking through the internet yesterday and saw an image of The Madonna of the Cat and POW, it hit me right between the eyes. It's like you painted a portrait of my family – like you KNEW us. I'm the child in your painting. Mum's the cat, and Dave is the Madonna.

The cat is wriggling free from the child and the mother is holding the child back – stopping it from going after the cat. Mum wriggled free from us and Dad tried to stop me from following her – that's why he told me she was dead. But it's wrong. You don't lie to your kids.

I was never allowed a pet – except when I was a baby, and I don't remember that. Every time I asked for one when I was growing up, Dave reckoned he was allergic to animals.

Kids need someone or something to love. Don't you reckon, Leo?

Matt

PS – I know where Mum is. I'm going to see her this weekend. Excited but nervous!

Chapter Thirteen

All week I fill my backpack with things to show Mum. There's the photo of my first day at school and my Year Six school report where my teacher said, "Matt is more than ready to start high school".

I find a drawing of Dave that won first prize in a Year One art competition. He looks like an alien, big head and pointy ears. It's not a great likeness, but you can sort of tell it's him. I pack a clock that I made out of a paper plate, and a mouse built from pipe-cleaners.

At tea on Friday night, I say, "I'm going to Troy's house tomorrow to do homework."

"Good. Make sure you work on that History assignment."

"Mrs D been dobbing, has she?"

Dave clatters his empty plate into the sink. "She rang me at work yesterday. She's worried that your work's slipping, that's all."

"Did you tell her why?"

"I would have if I'd known the reason myself."

How could you NOT know?

"Think about it, Dave." I storm off to my room.

―――――――――――――――――――――――

Hey Leonardo,

How did you feel when you met your mum again? You never had emails or phones, so you couldn't speak to her first and get some idea of whether she'd be pleased to see you.

I've got all this stuff to show Mum. Hope she likes my art. Was your mum proud of you, Leo? Luckily, I'm going to Mum's by train. If I had to go by horse and cart, like you, I'd never get there and back without Dave noticing.

He thinks I'm going to Troy's. I guess one good lie deserves another.

Matt

I'm up before Dave. I eat a quick breakfast and race out the door just in time to catch the bus to Melbourne.

I'm sitting behind a woman with a little kid who doesn't stop talking. We pass factories covered with red and purple graffiti. The kid keeps asking questions. "Who painted that, Mum? What does that word say? Are we there yet?" Finally, he falls asleep with his mother's arm around his shoulder. I get this urge to nudge him awake, to warn him how things can change. The mum smiles at me, and I feel my face go hot with guilt. Not all mums are the same. I hope that kid is okay — that things don't change for him like they did for me.

At Southern Cross Station the mother carries the son off the bus. I help her with the luggage. A lit-up board tells me that the train to Hillton is leaving from platform six in five minutes. I bolt.

As I leap onto the train, my legs are shaking. To calm myself, I slurp water from the bubbler at the end of the carriage. I drink too much and it makes me need to use the bathroom. I have to keep squeezing past an old lady with a trolley until eventually she asks, "Could we swap seats?"

"Sorry."

She sniffs. "Do you have a bladder problem?"

"No, I'm a bit nervous, that's all." And embarrassed.

When we stop at a station, I move to another carriage and grab a seat near the window. I close my eyes and try to steady myself. Mum can't see me in this state. I want her to think I'm cool, that I've grown up okay. I take deep breaths, filling my chest with air then exhaling as slowly as I can.

My heart stops racing and I open my eyes. I try counting sheep in the paddocks as we whizz by, but we're going too fast. I look at the people around me, and make up stories in my head about who they are and where they're going. I stop when a guy with a ring through his chin wants to know what I'm "gawking at".

The train slows and I can see a sign that says, "Hillton".

Ten of us get off the train and wait for it to leave the station before we cross to the platform that takes you into town. I count the cracks in the bluestone walls while we wait. I try not to think about where I'm going.

Mum's house is a five-minute walk from the station. Hillton isn't big. The house is just like she described on the telephone. It's hidden behind a fortress of huge peppercorn trees. Their thick trunks are lined up like soldiers. There's a cattle grid, too wide to jump. I clank across it, making sure my foot doesn't slip between the gaps. I following the long gravel-covered driveway. My breathing seems to get faster with every step. There's a massive rusty shed with a broken windmill towering over it, and a sign on the front that says. "Keep clear. Park this side." Maybe the shed is Mum's art studio.

The front fence is falling down and the gate sags off its hinges. It seems to be rusted in place, half open. Heart racing, I follow a stone path winding from the driveway towards the house. It leads to a wide verandah with two broken chairs and a tree stump stand between them.

Just next to the front door is a table with a half-drunk cup of coffee that still has steam rising from it. The coffee's black and thick like tar. I press the doorbell and wait but can't hear anything coming from inside the house. Not even the sound of the bell. Must be disconnected. There's a brown security door with mesh so thick that you can't see through it.

Inside the house, footsteps echo on wooden boards. I feel like a piano accordion with all the air squeezed out. She's here. I get to see my mother for the first time in ten years. All I've wanted to do since I found out she wasn't dead is to find her; ask her why she never came back; why she never even tried to visit. I want to know her – her paintings – what she's really like. In the back of my mind is all that stuff Dave told me about her, and the newspaper articles about those times she left me. She sounded fine on the phone. Not happy, not sad, not strange, not surprised; almost like she expected me to call.

The footsteps disappear. My stomach does a leap. I follow the verandah around the house, looking through windows. There are no lights on inside, but she has to be there. She knew

I was coming because she invited me. I heard her walking through the house.

Where is she? I knock hard on the door. No answer. I glance at the time on my phone. "Damn!" I knock harder. Still no answer. There's a metal echidna shoe scraper near the front door. I pick it up and use it to rap as loudly as I can. It's heavy. After three knocks I have to put it down again. Whoever is in that house *must* have heard me. My stomach is a blender, mixing everything together at high speed. Why won't she answer the door? Is she having one of her episodes? Another breakdown? Maybe she never got well? Is she lying to me too? Did she stay away because of Dave or because she never really loved me?

If I tossed that stupid shoe scraper through the window, that would get a reaction. Does even thinking that make *me* crazy?

When I fling my backpack on the ground, the zip splits open and my life over the last ten years spills out – all the stuff I chose so carefully to show Mum. Talk about an anticlimax. All this expectation for nothing – nothing but the hurt of knowing that no matter what she said on the phone, she doesn't really want me.

I should leave, head back to the station. But I have a right to be here. She's my mother. And I haven't done anything wrong. I wrap my hands around the mug. The coffee's still warm. I'm sure she's inside. Why is she doing this?

"I'm not going without seeing you," I yell. I look around, expecting to see neighbours peering over the fence, but there's no sign of anyone.

How can I make her show herself? I walk back up the stone path to the driveway and across to the shed. Maybe she's there, painting. I know this doesn't really make sense because the footsteps came from inside the house, but I don't know what else to do.

When I knock on the side door of the shed, nobody answers. It's locked. I walk around the back to what looks like the main entrance. It takes both hands to open the heavy sliding door.

The shed full of half-finished paintings, but each one is amazing. It makes me think of something I read that Leonardo said, "I have offended God and mankind because my work didn't reach the quality it should have."

Perhaps it's part of being a great talent – you never think that what you do is good enough – or complete.

I'm drawn to Mum's painting of a huge orange fireball on a black background. It looks hot and fierce, the way the anger against Dave still feels inside me. Wonder if he's the motivation behind this painting.

A white cat peeps from behind an easel.

I crouch down and call softly, "Here, puss."

She creeps out cautiously, followed by two tiny kittens that mew as they run after her. When they get close to me, they start spitting.

"It's all right. Don't be scared." I pat the mother cat, and she rubs against me purring. My legs cramp up, so I stand. When I look down again, the cats are gone. I start to wonder if they were really there in the first place.

Closing the sliding door behind me, I hurry back towards the front of the house. I call Mum's number. The phone rings inside, but she doesn't pick up. I wait for it to ring out. Try three times. Even if she came to the front door and told me to go away, that would be better than the silence. Then at least I'd have seen her.

I call Troy. "She's here," I tell him. "But she won't let me in."

"You're kidding?"

I kick the dirt. "Can't believe I've come all this way and now she won't even answer the door. She must know I'm here."

"What's her problem?"

I kick the dirt harder. "Probably never wanted me here. Just invited me to be polite."

Troy's voice comes through louder. "Maybe she's scared she won't be what you expected."

"I'm not expecting anything. I just want to see my mum." My voice cracks.

"Hang in there, mate."

"Yeah. Will you cover for me? I told Dave I'd be at your house."

"No worries."

"Thanks, Troy." I wipe my wet eyes with the back of my hand.

"So, what's it like where she lives?" asks Troy.

It's getting harder for me to talk. There's a lump in my throat that's getting bigger and bigger, a picture I keep getting in my head of Mum walking away and a small voice that whispers, "She doesn't want you. She never did."

"Gotta go. Tell you more when I see you." I hang up.

I give myself a minute to get it together, then phone Dave to tell him that I'm staying the night at Troy's.

After I've taken care of the phone calls, I go back to the front door of the house. There's still no answer when I knock. What else can I do? My stomach grumbles, calls for attention. I haven't eaten since lunch. I sit on the front steps and eat a chocolate bar from my pack.

Mum's in there. She's expecting me. She asked me here. So why doesn't she answer the door? Stuff her! I'll wait here all night if I have to.

Around half past five, the mosquitoes attack. They cover my arms with itchy red bumps. I've eaten everything I brought with me and I'm still starving. Didn't expect to be here so long.

A light goes on in the house, not sure where, it's probably in the kitchen. I pick up the shoe scraper and knock as loud as I can. No answer. Must be where I got my staying power. She's determined not to answer the door and I'm determined not to leave until she does.

I creep all around the outside of the house, peering in the windows. Each one is framed with cobwebs and a couple are cracked. It wouldn't be too hard to push the glass in, but I don't. All the curtains are drawn, and it's impossible to see which room the light is actually coming from. I wonder if she knows I am still here. I feel like a stalker. If anyone saw me, they would probably call the cops. But I'm not doing anything wrong. She invited me.

I smell food – something hot – smells like soup. It triggers a memory of a small boy sitting on a stool, watching his mother chop vegetables and toss them into a steaming pot. An involuntary tear slides down my cheek. The aroma of hot food wafts out to me, making my stomach growl. I shiver. The night air is moving in. An owl hoots, and I realise I've missed the last train home.

Hungry and cold, I retreat to the shed for the night. Now that I've come this far, I'm not going anywhere.

When it's too dark to even look at Mum's paintings, I curl up on a pile of sacks next to the cats and go to sleep, feeling even more confused than I was when I hopped on the bus this morning.

I'm woken by purring.

"Sorry, I don't have food for you. I don't even have anything left for myself." I pat the mother cat.

I'm just about to stand up, when the side door of the shed opens. It's Mum. It has to be.

I feel sick. I go hot then cold. Now that I'm finally about to come face to face with her, I need more time. I need to buy myself a few extra minutes. I lie down again and pretend to sleep; my right eye is open a slash so I can still watch.

She doesn't notice me at first. She sits in front of one of her paintings and runs her brush lovingly over the canvas. After nearly every stroke, she stops to look at her work – as if each stroke has to be perfect. Her dark braided hair stretches down her back like a piece of rope. She shakes it every now and then, and it swings and sways against her, like the pendulum in a grandfather clock. She doesn't seem to be aware of anything around her.

Suddenly, she stiffens. Her brushstrokes get faster, as if she's angry. The only time she stops is to dip her brush in the paint. She's totally focused on what she's doing, but I still won't be able to get out of either door without being seen.

I have a whole new set of questions for her. Why didn't

you answer the door yesterday, especially when you knew I was coming? Why did you pretend you weren't home? Don't you want me here? What did you expect me to do? Don't you care that I came all this way to see you? Do you really care about me? My brain flings these angry questions that almost reach my lips, but I keep my mouth closed tightly so they can't escape. I lie there watching.

After she finishes, she stands up. It's only a matter of time before I'm found out. Not sure what to do, I close my eyes again. Footsteps come closer. I can't stop myself from looking, but I'm not ready to talk to her yet. I still haven't worked out what I'm going to say. I peer out from under half-closed lids.

Material from her skirt brushes against me as she kneels down. The contact makes my skin tingle. Her perfume wafts through my memory, making my chest tight.

I open my mouth, ready to start my explanations, to justify why I stayed. That's how she's made me feel, that I'm the one who shouldn't be here, even though she invited me.

"Matt. You're still here?" She's calm – as if I hadn't spent hours yesterday knocking on her door, and she hadn't spent all that time pretending I wasn't there.

I don't get it. She saw me. Why wouldn't she answer her door?

A hand strokes my forehead. Bluff it, I tell myself. That's what Troy would do. I open my eyes fully and sit up. Hurt and disappointment get the better of me.

"You heard me knocking, didn't you? Why didn't you open the door?" These are not what I imagined my first words to my mother would be, but I can't stop them from spilling out.

She smiles. "I had the most awful migraine. Couldn't get out of bed. I'm really sorry about that. I know you came a long way to see me."

It doesn't make sense. If she couldn't get out of bed, who was sitting on the verandah yesterday, drinking coffee? It's too much. Too many lies. I want to put my hands over my ears and to yell at her. Stop it! No more lies!

"You'd better come to the house. I'll get you some breakfast.

I'm not much of a cook," she warns. "But I should be able to rustle up something."

Now that I'm about to finally step inside her house, I hesitate. I don't really know this person, even though she's my mother.

My stomach growls as if to say, "Don't be pathetic. I'm hungry."

I look at the back of her, her long dark hair stretching down to her waist. Is she how I pictured her? Yes. Is this how I thought our reunion would be, after being apart for ten years? No. I guess the kid part of me hoped she'd take me in her arms and tell me how much she missed me and how glad she is that I'm here. Clearly, that's *not* going to happen.

It's awkward. We sort of know each other, but we don't. She talks as if she has been my mother all along – like there isn't a ten-year gap between us. "Mind the step. Go and wash your hands before you eat." She points down the hallway. "First door on the left."

"Soup," I say. "You had soup last night." I wipe my eye, as the little boy memory creeps back into my head.

She turns to me. "Sorry, I ate all that."

Strange, the way she doesn't even mention that I spent the night in her shed, cold and hungry. She doesn't even seem embarrassed about it. But the tone of her voice is calm and reasonable – not a bit crazy.

She takes me into the lounge room and goes to make breakfast. I look around at the high ceilings and exposed beams. The place is old but arty, different. A huge spider works on a web that reaches across from one beam to another. Mum comes back.

"That's Charlie," she says. "He's my pet huntsman. Must think he's a trapeze artist. He's always swinging between the beams."

I smile. Dave hates spiders. So that would be one area where they didn't get along. Somehow, it makes me feel connected to her. We both like spiders.

"Great web, isn't it? I don't like to spoil his fun," Mum says.

"And I must admit, I'm not really a big one for housework."

"Me neither," I agree.

Mum laughs. She passes me a plate with toast and jam, and sits in the chair across from me. It's hard not to stare. What should I call her? Mum? Ms Matthews?

She seems to read my mind. "You don't have to call me Mum, you know. You're almost an adult now. You can call me Zora," she says.

Dave hates me calling him by his first name. "I'm all right with Mum," I say. I've wanted to call someone Mum for such a long time.

We stare at each other. The silence is too hard. I try to think of something to say. "Dad doesn't let me have toast for breakfast. Says I need something more substantial." How dumb does that sound?

"Well, that's your father for you. He would have read it in one of his books."

I think of the shelves at home, lined with volumes of useless information. "Has he always been like that?"

Mum nods. "Even before we were married, he had an amazing collection. *How to find the right woman, How to keep the right woman, How to be slim and successful.*"

"I think he still has that one."

We both laugh. Zora takes the empty plate from me and glances at her watch. "You'd better make sure you don't miss that train back to Melbourne. It's the only one on a Sunday."

But there's so much I still have to find out about her.

"Mum, why don't you live with us?"

"I can't."

"Why not?"

"It wouldn't work, Matt."

"Why not?"

"Because I'm sick."

"So Dad said. Big deal. Lots of sick people live with their families."

She clings to my arm. "Matt, do you know anyone who's

sick? I mean really sick?"

Her words scare me. What if her illness is terminal? What if she knows she's going to die and that's why she stayed away?

The only person I know who has really been sick is Troy's sister. "Troy's sister, Angie has allergies. She has to be careful with everything she eats. They reckon if she ate a peanut, she'd go into a coma and die."

"That's awful," says Mum. "The poor girl."

She still hasn't answered my question, not really. There's so much I need to know about me, about her, about her and Dave. Why don't they love each other any more? Why didn't she ever contact me? Why didn't she want me?

Mum takes my hand in hers and strokes my fingers. "Did you tell Dave you were coming?"

"No." I like the physical contact with her. "I rang him last night so he wouldn't worry, told him I was staying at a friend's place."

Mum pulls her hand away and clasps her fingers together on her lap. I pick up my backpack. "I brought some stuff to show you."

I pass her the photo of my first day of school. She hugs it to her chest. "It's gorgeous," she says. "Can I keep it?"

"If you like." I pass over the painting I did of Dave. "I got first prize for this."

"Really? Looks like you inherited some things from me. Have you kept up with your art?"

"Sort of. Dave's doesn't really like me painting." I wonder whether to tell her about the water tank, and decide against it. Don't want her worrying that Dave didn't bring me up right. Some people freak out when you mention police.

"Thanks for the card, by the way," I say.

"I wrote you one every birthday, you know. But that's the first I've ever sent. I kept every single card."

Why did she wait till now before sending one to me? "Can I see the others?" I ask.

"Sure." She gets up and leaves the room.

My head's stuffed with questions, but I don't want to scare

her off. I have to be careful what I ask.

Mum comes back with a brown paper bag that she holds out to me. "It might be best if you read these when you get home."

I look at my watch. "Guess I'd better go."

We both stand. She takes my hand again and holds it for a while. "I'm really glad you came. Promise you'll come again," she says.

I nod. "Bye, Mum."

"Bye, Matt."

Walking towards the station, I turn back hoping to see her wave from the verandah. But of course I can't see because of the peppercorn trees.

On the train I take out the cards. Every single one of them is handmade with one of her paintings on the front. There's so much written inside that they seem more like letters than birthday cards.

The first one says:

Dear Matty,

Happy sixth birthday, my sweet boy. I wish I could be there with you, holding you on my knee as you huff and puff out those candles like you did last year.

A mother should be there to celebrate her son's birthday.

How is school? I'm so sorry I wasn't there for your first day. Were you scared? Did Daddy take time off work to make sure you were okay? I bet he did. He always does everything right. He's always the perfect parent, not like me.

I hope you have a beautiful cake and lots of little friends to help you celebrate I would have given you a dinosaur party with a big Tyrannosaurus Rex cake – the sharp tooth, he was always your favourite.

You won't get this card because I've promised myself I won't send it. I just hope you can feel what's in my heart and know that your mother loves you.

Happy Birthday, my sweet angel.

Love Mummy.

I glance around the carriage, not sure what to say if someone asks why I'm crying. I brush away the tears, pretending they're specks of dust.

For ages I sit and stare out the window, can't bring myself to open another card. Not yet. There's already too much to think about.

Chapter Fourteen

Nobody's home when I get there. I lie on my bed, feeling calmer. I take out the next card and start reading.

Dear Matt,

Seven today, huh? I bet you've forgotten who I am by now. Did your father tell you I was dead? I hope so. I don't ever want you to come looking for me. I'm no good for you. I'm not good for anybody.

So, what have I done with myself in the year since you turned six? Not a lot, I'm afraid. Nothing to boast of, that's for sure.

I wonder if you'll have a party this year. I'm so tired at the moment, I don't think I could have made one for you anyway. I can't sleep again. My hay fever was really bad this week, so I had some drops – big mistake. It doesn't mix with my medication. Think I'll take a break from it. I need to paint.

Two hours sleep in the last three days. I must look a fright. You wouldn't want to see me like this.

It's been even harder this year. I've wanted to come to your school, to the house – to tell you I'm your mother and that I love you. But it wouldn't do you any good to know me. Look what I put your father through. Look what I did to you. Just goes to prove I should never have been a mother. Not that I didn't want you. I was so excited when I got pregnant. And I loved you from the moment you poked your grumbling little head into the world.

But being a mother was hard. Not because of you, my darling boy. You were the most adorable child. It was me. Normal people don't understand. Not that I'm making excuses for what I did. But it all just got too much for me that day.

And you can't talk to people about these things – about the terrible fear you have of what you might do to your own child.

You know I had to make your dad hate me so he'd let me go. I'm right, you know. I would have ruined your life. I hope I never do that.

Love, Mum

How could she ruin my life? She's my mother. Why is she bad for me? So what if things got too much for her to handle? I reckon that could happen to anyone. Why didn't she want me to look for her? I'm glad she changed her mind.

For ages, I stare at the letter. It makes no sense. What's so terrible about her? I know she's sick, but lots of people get sick and nobody takes their kids away. Mum doesn't seem that bad – odd maybe – but not terrible. I have to admit that spending the night in the shed wasn't great, but maybe the migraine came on, like she said. Maybe that's what the medication was for.

The first card was bright, but this one is dark – sad. I guess being without your kid would make you pretty unhappy.

Seeing her again has made all these snapshots in my head. I think they're memories from when I was little. It's like there's an electrical storm going on in there. Now I remember being cuddled by her like that kid on a train. I remember me as a little boy sitting on my mother's lap, resting my head against her softness.

It's so confusing. Like a jigsaw where some of the pieces are mixed with pieces from a similar puzzle and none of them quite fit together. None of it makes sense. Mum says she left for my own good, but that's a cop-out! Dave kept me away from her for my own good. But what about him? What did he do to make her leave and not return? The court said she could have "supervised visits", so how come she never did?

Someone has to know the truth about all this?

———————————————

Hey Leonardo,

Lies. Truth. How do you tell the difference?

Mum wrote to me every birthday when I was little – only she never sent the letters.

Ten years of not knowing how much she loved me – ten years of Dave's lies.

I get how people can find things hard to handle.

But finding her hasn't answered my questions like I thought it would.

If I couldn't write to you, Leo, and let it all out, I think I'd go crazy with all this.

Matt

Just after six, the front door slams.

"Matt, get here," Dave yells.

"What?" I appear in the kitchen doorway.

Dave stands hands on hips, briefcase tucked against his leg. "Where the hell have you been?"

"I rang you, Dave, remember? Told you I was staying at Troy's."

"Don't Dave me. I'm your father, and you're lying."

I turn my back and stroll into the living room. I throw myself casually onto one of the couches, not bothering to take off my shoes. It makes him angrier. He stands in front me, glaring. I stare back, wishing I had a cigarette I could dangle from my mouth – that would really make him mad.

Dave spits the words at me. "I know you weren't at Troy's. I went to pick you up there."

"Didn't Troy tell you I'd gone home?"

"Yes he did. But his mother told me you hadn't been there all weekend." A vein throbs in Dave's shiny forehead.

I turn away from him as if the whole subject's boring. "I ended up going somewhere else."

"Where, Matt? Where did you go?" He walks around the couch and tries to force me to look at him. "I've had it with your attitude. I want the truth. Don't lie to me."

I leap off the couch. "Me, lie to you? That's a joke. After all the lies you told me for the last ten years."

"Where were you?"

"Visiting my dead mother. You know, the one who died in a

car accident? And you talk to me about lying." I push past him and head to my room.

"Don't you walk away when I'm talking to you," Dave yells after me.

I slam the door and jam my bed against it. The door rattles as Dave tries to open it.

"Let me in, Matt. We need to talk," he shouts.

"No." He's not talking, he's yelling at me.

Dave stops rattling. "I said I'd go with you to see your mum."

"I don't want you there."

"You're not supposed to be alone with her. There's a court order. You broke the law."

"So what!" I toss my shoe at the door. Enjoy the thud.

"Matt, your mother could get into a lot of trouble over this."

"It was my choice."

Dave tries a different approach. "Come on, buddy. Let's discuss this."

"Why?" I yell back.

"Because I'm your father!"

I shove my bed out of the way and pull open the door with such force that Dave, who has been leaning against it, falls into the room. I run out, go to the bookcase and take out Dave's bible, *Sons and the Single Parent.* (Single by choice.)

Just because he has finally come clean about her not being dead, doesn't make what he did right. How can Dave think that one piece of truth makes up for all those lies?

I fling *Sons and the Single Parent* into the fireplace, light the corners with a match and watch it burn. Dave rushes in and reaches out to save the book, but I hold him back until the pages are well and truly alight, and there's no hope of saving it. "That's all you care about, Dave. Your precious book! Your pathetic quotes! You don't really care about me."

Dave turns, walks into the kitchen and sits at the table, holding his head in his hands. "Matt, why?"

"That's what I should be asking you."

Dave looks up. "Oh, Matt."

"I'm sick of the lies, Dave. Your lies!"

"I thought we'd been through all this. Didn't you read those newspaper articles?"

"So? You reckon they make up for everything?"

"Can't you see I had to protect you?"

"No! And by the way, I'm glad that stupid book's gone," I say. "It's the only thing you ever take notice of. You sure as hell don't listen to me."

I don't care what I say any more. When I burned that book, I went beyond the point of no return.

Chapter Fifteen

Another day off school – who cares? In the afternoon, Troy comes over to see what happened with Mum – and how things went down with Dave after he found I wasn't where I said I'd be.

He sits at my desk, swivelling in the chair, frowns when I tell him about Mum's migraine and how she seemed fine the next day.

"Maybe your dad was trying to protect you from her."

"That's what he says, but I reckon he was just trying to get back at Mum."

Troy rolls his eyes. "It's a protection thing for sure. Look at your dad, man."

I'm not sure where this is heading. "What about him?"

"He wraps you in enough cottonwool to clean the wax out of a dinosaur's ear. He's always trying to protect you from something. Remember how he wrote a note to the teacher in Year Five so you didn't have to play footy because he didn't want you getting hurt?"

"Yeah, I was quite happy about that. Wasn't keen to break bones either."

"What about that hat he made you wear to school whenever there were head lice going around?"

Wearing a beanie in thirty-degree heat wasn't much fun. "So, what's that got to do with anything anyway?"

"It proves this is all about protecting you."

"But I don't need him to. She's not some psycho."

"She's been in psycho hospitals, Matt. She might be dangerous."

"She's not dangerous. She's my mother!"

After Troy leaves I think about Dave's book – the one I burned. I really hated that book, but I guess burning it was a bit extreme.

I'm lying on the floor, looking up at the ceiling, when Dave walks in.

"Matt, it wasn't your fault, you know," he says. "It was her –

she couldn't handle being a wife or a mum."

"Why not?"

"I told you about her illness."

"Yeah, and? Sick people can still be parents. They have things called medicine these days."

Dave shakes his head. "I think it's time we went to see her together and got this sorted out once and for all."

You couldn't really tell from the train, but Hillton is like a place out of a history book. The roads have bluestone gutters, and the parks have lakes with pampas grass wafting in the breeze. A horse and cart clomps down the road, taking tourists wherever they want to go. A man in a top hat, with a microphone, tells people the history of the town. We pass a shop with a sign that says, "Welcome – come in and see how Granny lived as a girl." Dave laughs when I point it out.

"And nothing seems to have changed in town since then," he says. "Trust your mum to live in a place like this. Very atmospheric!"

The station is on the other side of town, so I missed most of this when I came by train. A pub advertises "Hillton sausages a specialty". It has an outdoor seating area at the front, where knives and forks wrapped in bright yellow serviettes threaten to take off in the wind. We stop at the only traffic light in town. On an electricity pole there's a poster of a missing grey cat. It's cute. I hope it gets found.

As we get closer to Mum's house, the muscle in the corner of Dave's eye starts to twitch. He stops the car outside the line of peppercorn trees, and we both get out.

"I don't want you to come with me. I have to do this by myself ..."

"But Matt, she–"

"No. She's my mother."

Dave slides back into the driver's seat, but sits with the door open. "You call if you need me."

"Yeah, I will."

He waves encouragingly as I walk up the stone path to the

house. I knock on the door. No answer, just like the first time I stood there. I knock again and yell, "Mum, are you in there?" When I look back to the car, Dave shrugs his shoulders and gestures for me to knock again. Still no answer. I try pushing the door open, but it's locked. I start to panic. At least there were sounds coming from inside the house last time I was here. This time there's nothing. What if she's had an accident – or worse? In my mind I see her lying helpless on the floor.

I run back to the car. "She's not there."

Dave opens the driver's door.

I don't want him coming. I want to do this myself. I rush my words. "I don't understand. I rang and told her I was coming, and now she's not here."

Dave points away from the house. "Check the shed."

I try the side door, but it's locked – so are the big sliding ones. The mother cat and her kittens mew from on the other side of the door.

When I get back to the car Dave's frowning. "I'm sure there's someone home. I saw the curtains move."

I run down the gravel path again, and knock on the door until my knuckles sting. I try the catch, but it's still locked. I want to bash the door down.

Dave comes to see what's going on. He yells out, "Open the door, Zora."

Suddenly, her face is at the window. She's there, watching us. I point to the front door. She mouths the words, "Go away."

"Let me in."

She shakes her head. She looks terrible, as if she hasn't slept for days. Her long dark hair hangs in greasy strands. She's got huge bags under her eyes and she looks terrified.

That's what scares me most. I'm her son. Why is she afraid of me? What does she think I'll do to her?

There's a sinking feeling in my stomach and I'm not sure why. It's a feeling of dread. I don't understand – Mum was a bit off last time, but not this bad. Did I say something to make her mad? Did I disappoint her? Maybe I didn't grow up the way she thought I would.

I shuffle back to the car.

Dave opens the door for me. "I'm really sorry," he says.

I climb into the passenger's seat and slam the door. "What's with her? If she doesn't want to see me, why doesn't she have the guts to say it to my face?"

"Maybe she doesn't want to hurt you."

"Yeah, well, this is the second time she's done it. She's not going to get another chance."

Dave puts a hand on my arm and looks at me intently. "I don't know what I can say to make it better," he says.

"You can't, Dave. I just wish I'd never come."

Dave starts the car and we drive off.

"You caught her on a bad day, that's all."

"I don't get it. First, she runs away and leaves me. Then she reckons she loved me all along – seems really pleased to see me. Then she blows me off again. I don't get it. What have I done wrong, Dave?"

Dave stops the car. "You haven't done anything, Matt. It's not you. It's her sickness."

"So she says, but what's she got? And why can't it be fixed?"

Dave hesitates, as if he's wondering how much to tell me.

"Come on! You promised, no more lies."

"You know how I told you about her mood swings when we first talked about her?"

I nod.

"That's part of her condition. It's called bipolar."

"What's that?"

"It means she has cycles in her brain. Sometimes she's manically happy and other times she's depressed and sad."

I pick at the seat cover. "Is she ever normal?"

Dave puts his hand on my arm. "When she's on her medication."

I look at it him. "Why can't we get her to take it?"

"I've tried. Everyone who loves her has tried. We've all been down that road with her so many times."

"You still love her?"

Dave nods. "In a way, I suppose I do. But I'd never let her

get close to me again. It would never work. On the medication, she's okay ..."

So it can be fixed! "What does she take?"

"It's called lithium. It helps even out the imbalances in her brain."

"Doesn't she want to get better?"

"She says that the medication stops her from feeling things – from being able to paint. She's made her choice. And there's not a damn thing you or I can do about it."

"But she's my mother."

"I know that. But you know what Rosenbaum says, 'You can't make someone else into the person you want them to be.'"

I feel like screaming. I've felt closer to Dave today than I have in ages and now he has to spoil it with another Rosenbaumism? To hell with Rosenbaum! I wish for once, he would tell me a Dave Hudson Original, something that comes from his own heart, and not out of a book.

"And what about you, Dave? What do you say?"

Hey Leonardo,

You said once, "He who is fixed to a star does not change his mind." Is that why Mum will always choose her painting over us?

Matt

Hey Leonardo

Mum is cruel. She's like a boy I saw in a park once. He lay on the ground with a butterfly perched on his hand. It sat there for a while and then suddenly, for no reason, the boy closed his hand and crushed it. Then he grinned.

It was awful. Holding that butterfly's life in his hands was just a game to him.

Is that all I am to Mum? Is that all any of us are?

Matt

From my desk, I grab her birthday cards and lay them out on the bed. I pick up the first one and hold it between my fingers, ready to rip it into a million pieces. That will teach her. See how she likes being torn into pieces and stomped on.

Dave walks in. "Don't, mate," he says quietly. "If you destroy them, you'll wish some day that you hadn't."

"I doubt that."

I think about the fifteenth birthday card, and the ones Mum never sent – the pieces of her from the past and a piece from the present. There will probably be nothing of her from the future, but I don't care. I take the cards I have read and start ripping. Dave tries to stop me but I push him away.

"Don't," I yell. "I have the right to do this."

Dave backs off and stands watching while I toss card confetti around.

When I finish I sit on the bed and cry. We stay like that for ages. I don't think Dave knows what to do. In the end he gets up and leaves.

"I'll give you space," he says.

I fall asleep on top of the trashed pieces of the past, and wake up at about 4 am feeling stiff and miserable. I climb into bed and pick up the cards I haven't read.

Reading Mum's words makes me feel better somehow. I'm sure she loves me – in her own way. Mothers have to love their kids, right? I wish Troy were here right now. He'd make one of his goofy comments like "What's not to love?" or "You've got a face that only a mother could love".

At 7.00 am Dave's at my door with bacon and eggs (not what Rosenbaum would recommend to start the day) and the hand-held vacuum cleaner. He puts breakfast on my desk, turns on the vacuum cleaner, and hovers it over the bits of paper. "Wait," I yell. "I might be able to put them back together."

"Come on." Dave grabs my empty wastepaper basket and sweeps all the pieces into it. "We'll do this at the dining room table. It will be easier."

I wolf down my breakfast and get dressed. We spend the next two hours bent over the table, separating the pieces of card into three piles of colour. Having seen and memorised the original images helps. We put the bits together like a jigsaw and paste them onto a piece of cardboard. There are obvious join lines, but eventually the cards are all in one piece.

Dave's being really cool about everything – considering all the stuff I said to him – and the fact that I destroyed his beloved Rosenbaum. I guess he's trying to make things right.

"I know you didn't sleep much last night. I'll drive you to school later, if you like," he says.

"I'll get the bus."

"I don't mind taking you. I'd rather make sure you're okay before I head off."

Sounds like his way of making sure I don't wag school again. "I'll be fine. You don't have to drive me." I try to stop my voice from shaking. "I guess I'll just go back to being what I was, before I found out I had a mother."

"It wasn't all bad, was it?"

"No, It wasn't."

I feel calmer than I have in ages. I guess we're starting to sort stuff out.

Hey Leonardo,

*You and I are **different**. Our mothers were **not** the same. Your paintings are full of little kids with curious smiles; wearing the confidence of their mother's "everlasting" love. To paint like that, you had to know what it felt like.*

Matt

Chapter Sixteen

At school Troy ambushes me as soon as I get off the bus.

"How did it go? What was she like? Did you talk?"

Where do I start? I choose my words carefully, try to keep it impersonal, contained. Try to stop the overwhelm from grabbing hold of me again. "We didn't talk."

"She wasn't there again?"

"She was there." The memory of her fear makes me sick in the stomach.

"What? Matt, what happened?" Troy stands in front of me like he's trying to shield me from the other kids – so they can't see I'm upset.

"She was terrified. She wouldn't let me in the door." The words come out in a whisper.

"What was she scared of?"

"Me."

He shakes his head. "That's crap. You're her son."

The memory makes me cringe all over again. "You should have seen her face in the window. Like I was an axe murderer trying to break into her home."

"You're kidding. What's with her?"

"She's sick. She has this thing called bipolar."

He nods, like he knows what it is, which he probably does seeing as his mum's a counsellor. "Isn't there something you can take for that?"

I scuff my shoe on the asphalt. "Not if you want to be an artist. Not according to the way she thinks."

The bell goes for the start of class. I sidestep Troy and run to my locker. I've had it with talking about Mum, thinking about Mum, wondering why she made the choices she did – why she doesn't even seem to know how much she has hurt me – and doing it over and over again.

After school, I'm doing my homework at the kitchen table

when there's a knock at the door.

"Door's open, Troy," I yell.

Slow footsteps creep down the hallway. They don't sound at all like Troy's size nine Blundstones. I get up from the table.

"Mum!" At first, when I see her standing there, I'm shocked. Then I get mad. "What are you doing here?"

"Sorry about the other day, Matt. I really am. You just caught me at a bad time."

Not much of an apology. She's making out it's my fault. "You could have at least answered the door."

"I couldn't, Matt. Not the way I was." She shoves a red and blue striped plastic bag towards me. "Here, I brought you these."

"What are they?"

Mum smiles. "I know it's a bit late. But these are all the birthday presents I bought for you over the years."

"What if I don't want them?"

"Come on, Matt," she coaxes. "Aren't you even a little bit curious?" She pulls out a Lego robot. "I got you this the year you turned six. What do you think?"

She crouches on the floor and walks it towards me. It reminds me of Troy's Frankenstein monster walk. The thought makes me grin.

"See, I knew you'd like it," she teases.

I'm not quite ready to forgive her yet. "Mum, we need to talk."

"Later. Let's have some fun first."

She sits on the floor in the hallway and takes other toys from the bag, an easel, paints, shoes, a clock radio, rollerblades and a spitting dinosaur.

The dinosaur has three horns on top of its head like a Triceratops. Mum pulls a plastic cap off one horn and takes the toy to the kitchen sink where she fills it up with water. She puts the dinosaur on the floor in front of me. "Turn it on." She's like an excited kid.

I flick the switch. The dinosaur plods down the hall. Mum pushes a button on the side of its head and the dinosaur spits water. A splash hits me in the eye.

Mum laughs. "Can't believe the batteries still work. I bought this nine years ago."

She runs down the hall, turns the dinosaur around and walks it back towards the kitchen. She looks at me sadly. "I guess you've grown out of most of them. They'll only clutter up your room anyway." She starts to put the toys back in the bag.

I take them from her. "Thanks, Mum."

"Friends again?" She smiles brightly.

"Mum. It's not that simple."

She slumps into a chair, stops being the excited kid. "I know it's not that simple, Matty. But I'm really sorry I hurt you. I'm sorry for all the times I've hurt you."

It's hard to keep up with these sudden changes in her. Nothing about her is simple.

"Why, Mum? I don't understand any of it. I don't understand why you picked art over us. Can't you have both?"

She tries to hug me. "It doesn't work for people like me, Matt. I don't get to have it all."

I pull away. "Why not, Mum?"

She won't let me go. "Because of my sickness."

"Dad told me about bipolar."

She nods, but doesn't get mad like I thought she would.

"Troy says lots of people who are bipolar still have families – and they take meds so they can be normal. Why can't you?"

She steps back and looks into my face. Her voice is soft and uncertain. "Matt," she says. "You can't just take one course of tablets and make bipolar go away. It's not like having the flu. It's like a terminal illness. You have to take the tablets forever. For every day of your life."

So? I don't get it. "Why wouldn't you take them if it meant you could be well?"

She's close to tears. "But I can't paint the same when I'm on my meds. I don't have the intense creative spark, the inspiration. When I'm not on them I feel like I'm living. It's hard for me to control how I feel and sometimes, I even do things that I really wish I hadn't."

I almost say, "Like leave your child in a shopping centre." Instead, I bite my lip to stop the words spilling out.

"But at least I feel things fully." A tear drops down her cheek.

"You seem okay now, Mum."

Mum frowns. "I'm a bit like your friend's sister in a way, the one with the allergies," she says. "Angie has to think about everything she eats, and I have to think about everything I do. It's hard for me to know what's real and what's not. I have to consciously work out if what I'm doing and feeling is real or just some part of a high or low cycle."

I'm still confused. She looks normal – like any mother trying to help her son understand something. "Are you like that all the time – even now?"

She nods. "Even sitting here talking to you, I'm thinking, is this the right thing to do? Is it appropriate? Am I saying the right things? Is this how normal people behave? I don't know. I can't tell."

"There must be something you can do, some treatment."

She shakes her head. "I just feel so bad for hurting you again."

"These cycles, do they last long?"

"It depends. Some people only go off the rails now and then. But I'm what they call a rapid cycler. It means I get them all the time – that's why it's hard to work out what's real and what's not. It all seems real to me."

I think of the night sky. I like to pretend the constellations are real. I pretend that Sirius really is a dog and the Seven Sisters belong to him. But afterwards, I always know it's all in my imagination. I try to understand what it must be like for Mum – not to be able to tell the difference, to be scared of yourself and what you might do.

"I can't imagine what it would be like not to just do things," I say. "Sometimes what I do works out and other times it doesn't. But most of the time it doesn't really matter either way."

"It's not like that for me," says Mum. "I can do terrible things if I'm not careful."

For the first time, I see how brittle she is. "So why don't you take the meds?"

"I used to. But it doesn't work for me, for my art. Seeing things in such an intense way, is what makes my paintings so deep, so unique."

She looks beautiful when she talks about her work. Her cheeks dimple and her eyes shine with a glow that lights her whole face. I wonder if there will ever be anything in my life that makes me that happy.

"Couldn't you take less medicine when you're painting?"

Her face clouds over. "If you don't take the right dose, it doesn't work. Matt, I really am sorry. I came here today to try and make it up to you. I want you in my life. I'll do whatever it takes." She reaches into her handbag and takes out a bottle of tablets. "Lithium," she says. "I'll try meds again. I'll go back on these, if you'll just give me another chance."

It overwhelms me. I've never had anyone prepared to make such a sacrifice for me before. "But what about your painting?"

"You're my son. You matter more."

What if she changes her mind? What if she decides to leave me again? What if I get used to her being in my life again? "I don't know, Mum. Why do you want to do this now?"

"I think I'm stronger. And I'm not going to risk losing you again. I'll be all right, you know." She holds up the tablets. "As long as I keep taking these."

I don't know if any of this is a good idea, but Dad said she was okay when she was on her medication.

"Come on, Matty." Mum grabs my arm. "Let me make it up to you."

"I guess it would be cool to catch up on weekends and things."

"I've got a better idea. Wait here." She runs out the front door.

105

I send the robot down the hall after her. I look through the bag of toys she gave me – all the stuff I would have loved when I was little.

Mum comes back carrying two suitcases. "I'm going to stay for a while. You'll get to know me a lot quicker that way."

I just about choke. Dad will have a fit. Can I say, "No?" Do you say things like that to your own mother? "What about Dad?" I say.

Mum seems to have already thought of an answer. She says quickly, "If he knows you really want me here, he won't throw me out."

I don't even know if I'm ready to have her here. I don't even know her – not really. "I'll have to ask him first."

"Of course. Why don't you call him now?"

I don't know what to do.

Dave won't like it. But she's my mother, I owe her this chance, don't I? But what if she goes weird on me like she did up at her house? What if I can't deal with her? The whole idea scares the life out of me.

I need to buy myself time to think. Dad vs Mum. This is a mega step. "I can't do this over the phone, Mum. This is something I have to tell Dad in person."

"You do what you need to do, Matty. I'll be here waiting when you get back. You know I love you," she says.

I grab my bike from the back verandah and head off. Completely distracted, I nearly ride straight into a lamppost, only a girl about my age yells just in time, "Watch out."

Once I get to Dad's office, I ride around the block a couple of times before I go inside, still trying to get things straight in my head.

Finally, I decide what to do. I lean the bike up against the front of Dad's work and walk in. I need to get to know Mum better. She is my mother.

Dad's between customers. He looks up from his paperwork and smiles at me. "Hi, buddy," he says. "Don't see you round here too often."

Sitting across from him, I have a sick feeling in my stomach – the sort you get when you know you shouldn't be asking for what you're about to ask for.

"I was wondering if you'd mind if we had someone living with us for a while." I shift in my seat.

Dad laughs. "Troy been kicked out of home, has he? I always knew it would happen eventually."

I take a deep breath. "Actually, it's Mum," I say as casually as I can – even though I feel my face burning. "She's at the house. Wants to stay for a while and get to know me better."

Dad goes instantly purple and swallows as if he's trying to control what's going to come out of his mouth. He doesn't say anything.

"So, what do you think, Dad?" I ask tentatively.

"I think she's manipulative and selfish, and I'm not having that woman in my house."

His reaction is worse than I expected, but it comes as no surprise, not after what he's said before about her. I have to make him understand. I have to take this chance. "But Dad, she's my mother."

Dad's eyes dart back and forth. His fingers tap the desk. I've never seen him look so scared. "Oh, Matt. Look what she did to you – to all of us."

"Please, Dad. She's going back on her medication. She promised."

"But for how long?"

I try to sound confident. "She seems pretty serious about it."

"She always is," says Dad, bitterly. "But it doesn't last. Before long she'll be thinking she doesn't need it any more. Then she'll be stuffing us around again. Look what she did to you when you were small, dumped you in a shopping centre – anything could have happened to you. There's a reason the court wouldn't allow unsupervised visits. She can't be trusted."

"But I'm not a little kid. She can't hurt me now."

Dad snorts. "Huh!"

I don't blame him for being angry, but Mum's not that person any more. She seems to be in control. I have to give her a chance. The only way to convince Dad that this is a well-thought-out decision is to stay calm, show him that I know what I'm doing, that everything will be all right. "Maybe she's changed. Please, Dad? For me?"

"Forget it, Matt. It's not going to happen. It's *for you* that we're not having her in the house."

Why is he being so unfair? "Fine, tell her yourself then. She's at the house. She's got her stuff there already."

Dad stands up. "I will tell her. I'll tell her exactly what I think of her and her scheming."

I can't face Mum – can't face her disappointment or mine. I run out, jump on my bike and race it at full speed round and around the block till the perspiration and tears make it hard for me to see. I'm surprised at how fiercely I want her to stay. What if she goes back to Hillton and I never see her again?

When I arrive home later, Dad has his nose buried in a new book, and there's no sign of Mum.

"I hope you're happy." I stomp to my room, so wild I punch the wall. I wait for Dad to come thumping in and tell me off.

But he doesn't say a word.

Dad tries to make it up to me by letting me pick takeaway for tea. As if that changes anything? I barely speak to him while we chew on pizza. I picture Mum's face when Dad told her she couldn't stay. It makes the crust stick in my throat.

After tea I go to the water tank with Troy. He has new cans and wants to paint, but I'm not feeling inspired. "I'm so sick of Dad," I tell Troy. "He doesn't listen, doesn't care what I think."

Troy flicks his ear with a blade of grass. "It's typical. Parents want us to act grown up, but they still treat us like kids."

"Don't know how much more of this I can take."

Troy throws a piece of grass at me. "Come to my house for the weekend. Have a break from reality."

"Thanks, think I will."

"As long as you don't mind Angie and her noisy friends."

"At least they're normal."

Troy laughs. "Well, sort of."

Dad's sitting at the kitchen table when we get back – the empty pizza box in front of him. He has his "we need to talk" look on his face.

"Catch you later." Troy hurries out the front door.

I pretend I don't realise Dad wants to talk. I take the pizza box out to the garbage bin, then sneak in the back door and go to my room.

Hey Leonardo,

They're tearing me apart. It's like my skin is paper thin and my insides are being ripped in two. Why does Dad hate Mum so much? We all do stuff we wish we hadn't.

I feel like your Baroncelli, the guy they hanged for murdering Lorenzo the Magnificent's brother.

I'm hanging there, waiting for someone to let me down, stop the pain. But I don't reckon they're going to. Don't think either of them will ever give the other a fair go.

Why can't all this just go away? Why can't my life go back to what it was when I thought Mum was dead?

Matt

Chapter Seventeen

I'm packing my stuff for the weekend at Troy's when there's a knock at the door. "Just a minute." I zip my pack and run down the hall.

It's Mum. My heart thumps. She's standing on my front doorstep.

"Hi, Matty. How are you?"

I don't know what to say. "Mum, you can't stay here."

I'm relieved that she's still around, that she never went back to Hillton. But I can't shake that feeling I got when I saw her through the window and she wouldn't let me into her house. It's as if she's two people. Sometimes she's the one with the uncombed hair and sad eyes. Then she's the woman with the bright eyes and big smile standing in front of me.

"I know, I can't stay with you. I've rented the house next door."

My stomach tightens. I feel sick. "What does Dad think?"

"He's not ecstatic about the idea." Mum shrugs.

"I'm amazed he even rented the place to you."

"He didn't. I went direct to the owners."

I hang my head. "Sorry I couldn't talk him into letting you stay with us."

"Don't worry, Matt. I'll have more room to paint if I have a whole house to myself."

She said she wasn't going to be painting because she's on her medication. I don't say anything.

I text Troy to tell him that I can't make it for the weekend after all. I also ask him if he thinks she lied about taking her meds.

Troy texts back:

She never said she wouldn't paint just that the pills make it hard.

He's right. Having Mum living next door means I can get to know her without Dad interfering for a change. He can't stop me spending time with her, can he?

Hey Leonardo,

Now that Mum has moved in, I feel like I'm stalking her – my own mother. Even when I'm not watching her, I'm wondering what she's doing.

Is she thinking of me too?

Is she glad we found each other?

How do I stop her from leaving again?

Matt

It's nearly two weeks since Mum moved in next door. Every night I peer through her kitchen window and try to guess what she's cooking for dinner. Tonight the window is open, and I smell burnt toast.

After dinner, she waters the plants and hums to herself. She sounds happy.

Dad walks through the door and sees me watching her. "Won't last." He flings his briefcase onto the floor.

"You're just grumpy because she did something you didn't want her to." Yesterday when we went to check out the local art gallery, Mum told me that the real reason things didn't work out between them was that Dad wanted to control her all the time."

Dad rolls his eyes.

I get home from school next day to find Mum singing "Don't Cry for me Argentina" at the top of her voice. It's so loud that the neighbours are staring over the fence. Mum doesn't seem to care. Just goes on singing.

When I'm doing my homework, I open my window to listen to the sound of her: the whoosh of the vacuum cleaner, the whirr of the washing machine and the click of high-heeled shoes on polished boards. Mum being busy.

The phone rings.

"I'm baking a cake," Mum says when I pick up. "To celebrate

us finding each other. Why don't you visit in a half an hour or so?"

I finish my homework, and head over.

She doesn't answer the door, but it's open.

Mum's in the kitchen, sobbing. "I don't know why it didn't rise," she sniffs, pointing to a flat chocolate cake, so flat that it could be a biscuit tin lid.

"Don't worry about it, Mum. We'll use it as a frisbee."

That makes her smile. "It's just that you're always telling me what a good cook Troy's mother is," she says.

I put my arm around her. "She can't paint like you."

She pulls away. "But I don't want to be a painter. I want to be your mother."

"You are. It doesn't matter if you can't cook. I don't care."

She hugs me. "You're so sweet, Matty. Just like your father when I first met him."

When Dave and I are having tea, I tell him about the cake.

"You should have seen it. Poor Mum got so upset, but it was funny. It looked more like a chocolate pizza."

Dad looks serious. "I hope she's still taking her medication."

"It was just a cake, Dad. You don't have to make such a big deal."

He shrugs. "I'm just wary. I've seen the signs before."

Why does he have to pick fault with everything Mum does? She's trying so hard. She even moved down here to be near me. What more does he want from her?

"Dad," I say, exasperated, "she was upset because she wanted the cake to be perfect. That's all."

"We'll see," he says. "We've got your school play tomorrow. See what she gets up to there."

The school play is *Antony and Cleopatra*. Tina is Cleopatra so Troy wanted to be Antony, but he forgot to audition. He'd have done all right as Antony. Instead, they gave the part to a scrawny guy in Year Twelve with a really boring voice.

The play is the first school thing of mine that Mum has been to. She looks amazing in a green and gold dress. The way she hovers, hesitating in the entranceway with the glare of lights behind her, makes her look kind of surreal – other-worldly, like Leonardo's *Benois Madonna*.

Mum flits between the rows of parents and kids like a Christmas beetle. She seems so happy to be there, enjoying herself. I don't think she gets out much.

Dad is serious, watching her as if he's waiting for her to slip up.

Even though Mum looks happy, there's a sharpness in her eyes that makes her confidence seems fragile. Like if you said something nasty to her, the facade would fall away. As long as nobody is mean to her, she'll be fine.

Before the play starts, Mum chats to Mr Madden.

"Better see what she's up to," says Dad.

He takes off and comes out on the other side of the crowd.

Troy's late as usual. I wave when he walks in. He ditches his parents and climbs over the rows of people to take an empty seat next to me.

"Do you mind if Mum sits there?" I ask. It's the first school event ever that both my parents have been to.

"Sure!" Troy moves to the seat two spots away.

Mr Madden walks to the stage at the front of the room. When I look around I've lost sight of Mum.

Dave comes back. His face is flushed and anxious. "Where is she? Have you seen her? Where's your mother?"

"Don't worry, Dad. She probably went to the bathroom. She'll be okay."

Dad fidgets in front of the seat that has been left for him. "I knew this was a bad idea," he says. "We should never have brought her."

"I wanted her to come, Dad. She's my mum."

Mr Madden taps the microphone. "Quiet, please."

People bustle around, taking the closest seat. Then I spot Mum near the front row. She climbs onto the stage and whispers something in the headmaster's ear. Mr Madden smiles at her and turns back to the microphone.

"Before the performance starts," he says, "I'm delighted to inform you that the well-known artist, Zora, who happens to be the mother of one of our students, has just announced her intention to donate $10,000 towards our arts program at school. Thank you, Zora. I'm sure many students will benefit from your generous contribution."

I clap loudly. So does Troy. Dad sinks lower in his chair. "What's wrong?" I ask Dad.

"Matt, where do you think she's going to get that kind of money?" "You've been to her house. Does she seem rich to you?"

I hadn't thought about it. I just know I'm proud to have Mum back in my life. Why can't Dad be happy for me? "Maybe she sold one of her paintings or something. You could be pleased for me, Dad. This is my school. And you've never done anything like that."

Dad groans. "Don't you see, Matt? This is just another one of her antics."

"Why do you have to doubt everything she does?"

People are looking at us.

Dad puts a finger to his lips and hisses, "Matt, I've known her a lot longer than you."

Whose fault is that?

The play starts. A woman behind nudges me to be quiet. I ignore her. "Yeah well, I reckon it's no wonder she didn't stick around the first time. She wouldn't have got much support from you."

Dad puts his hand on my arm and says softly, "You don't know, Matt, you were only a kid."

At least Troy's happy. He gets to perve on Tina all night. "Best play I've ever seen," he says at the end.

"Would have been if my parents hadn't ruined it."

_____

Hey Leonardo,

Not sure that fame is all that it's cracked up to be.

Doesn't seem to have done much for Mum.

Probably just as well you never had kids – trying to learn to live in your footsteps.

I'm totally conflicted. I'm proud to be an artist like Mum, but terrified on so many levels.

Matt

Chapter Eighteen

I'm a celebrity at school now. Great, just what I wanted. Everyone wants to know about my "famous" mum.

Troy reckons it's awesome. "Fame helps you land hot chicks," he says.

I don't want a chick, hot or otherwise. There's so much to sort out already without making my life more complicated.

"How come we haven't seen her at school before?" says Jacinta Riley.

"You too weird for her?" asks Reece Burns.

I escape to the library at lunchtime and recess. Man, I'm sick of all the razzing and their questions that I don't have answers to.

Hiding behind a giant book on Renaissance Art works for a while. Then Lisel Power peeps out from behind the Countries of the World shelves and asks, "What's it like having a mum who's rich and famous?"

"No talking in my library," says Mr Lancel, our "rules are rules" librarian.

Lisel Power pouts at him and walks out. Thanks, Mr Lancel.

After school, Mum takes me into town to enrol me in Steve Bridges's art classes, the ones I'm supposed to have started already, but haven't got around to because of everything that's been happening around here lately.

Steve, normally Mr Cool, goes bright red when Mum introduces herself. He even stammers. "I c-c-ca-a-n-t b-believe, you're Zorina, and y-your Matt's M-u-m."

Mum puts an arm around me. "Sure am."

Steve grins at me, "I can see where you get your talent from."

Mum signs me up for the classes then does a tour of the shop. She takes a set of twenty-four watercolours off the shelf. "Time we got you some decent paints," she says as she hands over the money to Steve.

I pick the box up off the counter. "Thanks, Mum. You didn't

have to do that."

"I wanted to. All those times I've missed out on being able to buy my little boy presents."

I cringe. Steve laughs. "N-not so little," he says.

"What are you doing tonight?" Mum asks me.

I shrug. "Probably homework."

"No, you're not. I'm coming over. You need to learn how to use those paints the right way."

"That would be great, Mum."

"I'll show you how to do a proper wash."

Dad has never bought me paints, let alone encouraged me to use them. It really is going to be cool having Mum around.

It's 10.30 pm and I am still sitting at the kitchen table, pretending I've got more homework to do, even though I finished it about an hour ago. I can't concentrate. My eyes keep wandering out the window to her house. There are no lights on. Mum must have gone out – must have forgotten.

At first I'm really disappointed, then I start to wonder if maybe she did it deliberately. Maybe she's testing my resilience. Maybe she's testing to see if I have the guts to be a painter.

You do need guts for that sort of thing. You put your work out there for people to trash. It's like laying a part of yourself on the ground for everyone to walk over.

I wonder if that's why Leonardo never finished anything. Perhaps people rubbished his work before it was even completed?

You need more than talent. Do I have what it takes to be an artist?

———————————————————————

Hey Leonardo,

What sort of a teacher was Verrocchio? Did he help you keep going – even when people didn't like what you painted?

I read somewhere that he was always broke because he had to feed and clothe his students. Don't reckon any of our teachers are that dedicated.

Mrs D is being a regular pain at the moment. Wants to know where my "Da Vinci letters are.

I'm not lying when I say I've written them, but seriously, most of this stuff is none of her business.

Matt

I accidentally let it slip at breakfast that Mum promised to come over and didn't turn up.

Dad has *that* look on his face again.

Mum rushes in after breakfast.

"I'm so sorry, Matty," she says. "I had one of my terrible migraines." That explains the darkness. "I should be right for tonight. That's if you don't have anything else on."

While she's here, Dad doesn't say anything. He hides behind his newspaper and pretends he's not listening.

But after she leaves, he says, "Don't hold your breath, Matt. She's notoriously unreliable."

He should talk! He's the one who lied to me for ten years.

I know she'll come this time.

My first class with Steve Bridges is a blast. He does a demo watercolour first, of ducks on a pond. He shows me how to build the layers step by step. It's amazing.

"It would be so cool to be an artist," I say. "Maybe go to uni."

"I went there," says Steve.

"I bet you learned heaps."

Steve laughs. "Learned more about how to party than how to paint. It doesn't make you rich," he says. "Not unless you're famous like your mum. Working in art shops like this is cool because you get your materials cheap. But I'd rather be painting full time."

"Me too."

Steve laughs. "You have to at least finish school first."

"Yeah." He might not be famous, but he's an unreal painter, and at least he gets to do what he wants. He wears what he wants and has a ring through his nose. His hair is halfway down his back. He has to tie it back when he paints. Dad doesn't like long hair on men. Says most blokes don't look after long hair properly and it ends up looking revolting. That's one of the reasons he never wanted me doing Steve's art classes. Worried he'd be a bad influence.

At least Mum isn't like that. She wouldn't care if a person had two heads and a tail. She said the other day that you have to look at people as if you are going to paint them. When you're painting someone you can't just paint what you see. You have to peel back the layers and look at what's really on the inside. I like the idea of that.

I reckon that's what Leonardo did with the *Mona Lisa*, only he didn't quite reveal everything. Or maybe his subject kept part of herself hidden.

After Steve does his demo, we talk about viewpoint. He says, "Before you even start painting, you have to decide your angle, your perspective, and what part of the object you're going to focus on."

That's what I like about painting. You get to make your own choices, and nobody can tell you that what you're doing is wrong.

I run home, my head spinning with all the stuff Steve taught me. I can't wait to tell Mum all about it.

Only she doesn't show. Again!

Chapter Nineteen

Next morning at breakfast, I'm in a foul mood. I'm sure Dad knows why, but he doesn't say anything. No apology from Mum this time. What now?

It's hard to concentrate at school. My mind keeps coming up with scenarios as to why Mum never showed, and none of them are good.

I drift through the morning in a haze. Don't even react when Mrs D makes one of her dry comments about my incomplete History homework.

In Science we pair up to work on an assignment. Troy and I decide to do ours on the solar system, on Pluto, and how it got demoted from being a planet.

"Can we work at your place?" asks Troy.

"If you want, but don't expect chocolate cake."

"I won't. But it should be quieter without Angie and her friends."

As the school bus pulls up near our house, I see a row of cars parked outside.

"Hey, look Matt!" Troy points to a sign on the front gate. "Garage Giveaway. Free to the Needy."

A woman gets out of a white Mercedes. She doesn't look needy. She's dressed in a cream suit and she's wearing dangling gold earrings.

Mum's there, dressed up in one of her flowing dresses, smiling brightly. She looks like a celebrity greeting her fans, like she's waiting for someone to roll out the red carpet.

She hands over my TV to the woman in the white suit. MY TV!

"Mum, what are you doing?" I rush forward.

"Having a Garage Giveaway. Isn't it fun?" Mum's face is shiny. "Out with the old, and in with the new. That's my motto," she tells the woman carrying the TV.

Mum nods at the peeling weatherboards and sunken verandah on our house. "A complete makeover. That's what this place needs – inside and out." She turns to Troy. "Don't you agree?"

I race over to the rich woman who is putting my TV into the back of her car. "Excuse me. Look, I'm really sorry. But that's mine."

"But that lady said I could have it."

Doesn't she think it strange that someone wants to give away brand-new stuff? I feel my face go red, and stare down at my shoes. "Mum didn't realise it was mine."

"I see." The woman reaches into the boot, picks up the TV and thrusts it at me. "You'd better have it back then."

"I'm really sorry," I mumble.

I carry the TV back to the house. Maybe I should have just let it go. For once Troy doesn't have anything to say. His mouth and eyes are round like egg rings.

When I get to the front door, Mum confronts me, hands on hips, her face creased with confusion.

"What are you doing with that?" she asks.

"It's mine, Mum."

She looks surprised. "But that lady was so lovely. I thought you'd want her to have it. I'm getting you a new one anyway."

"It was practically new, Mum. Dad got it for me last Christmas."

Mum's hands slip off her hips. "Was it?" she says. For a moment she looks puzzled then her face brightens again. "Well, I want you to have one that I bought for you. I'm going to get you all new stuff."

The kitchen table is set up on the front lawn. My telescope's still there, and my digital camera. Not much of my stuff has gone.

Mum's acting so strange. I want to ask her what she gave away, but I don't want to make her mad. "Garage Giveaway just started?" I ask.

She nods. "But it was going so well. I gave your watercolours to a lovely young boy. He was thrilled."

"But Mum you only just brought them for me. I hadn't even used them."

"Chill Matt. I'll buy you some more, even better ones. That boy was so grateful."

So was I when she bought them for me. This is the weirdest behaviour ever.

"The lad was going to take the telescope too, but couldn't carry it on his bike."

Shame about that!

I deep breathe, force myself to stay calm "So what else did you give away?"

"A couple of your father's daggy old suits."

No loss there. "Anything else?"

"Not that I can think of. But it doesn't matter. Like I told you, out with the old, in with the new."

"But who's going to pay for it all?"

Troy picks up my telescope and starts to carry it back into the house.

"You sound just like your father." Mum pouts. "But since you ask, I'm going to pay for it."

"What with? I thought you didn't have any money." And she promised $10,000 to the school.

"Not yet. But I will. The National Gallery's going to buy two of my new paintings."

I hadn't thought of that. Of course she'll have money if she sells some of her work. I want to be happy for her, so I paste on an enthusiastic smile. "Really? That's fantastic! Which ones?"

"Well, they haven't exactly signed on the dotted line yet," Mum smiles at me. "But I'm sure they will – when they see them."

"What new paintings?" whispers Troy, who is back outside, collecting more gear. "She hasn't done any since she's been here, has she?"

I glare at him and then turn back to Mum. "Come on, Mum. We'd better put this stuff back."

I carry CDs and the gear from my wardrobe into the house. Troy picks up a box full of plates and cups and follows me.

It's not until Mum's gone that I remember I haven't asked

her where she was last night. Then again, I think I already know the answer.

The next day at school Troy asks, "Is your mum okay?"

"What do you mean?" I ask.

"That was seriously bizarre behaviour, man. Giving your stuff away like that. I'd be pretty ticked off with my mum if she tried that sort of thing."

I shrug. "Yeah, well, I don't think she realised what she was doing."

"Your mum sure is a strange one." Troy grins.

I can't see the funny side. It's easy for Troy to smile. The biggest issue he faces is whether Sunday roast is going to be lamb or pork.

"Shut up, idiot. Who asked you?" I say.

"Nice one. Why are you giving me a hard time? I'm not the one who tried to sell your stuff. I'm only trying to help."

I don't want his help! I just want everything to be normal, for him to leave me alone. But I can't say it. Troy has been my best friend forever, he's the one who helped me through all this stuff when I first found out she was alive. I turn away.

"What's happened? I thought everything was working out well for you guys."

"I dunno. I've never seen her like this."

"What, off her tree?"

"Shut up!"

We're sitting behind the shelter shed. I pick up a stone and fling it at the wall, wait for the thud.

Troy stands up. "Sorry, but it's true."

I feel the tightness in my stomach. The feeling that has come and gone ever since I read those articles in the paper and the memories started coming back to me. I wish I could ignore it, but it's like a thread that somebody is drawing tighter.

There's a voice in the back of my head that keeps whispering, "Maybe Dad's right. Bringing Mum into our lives isn't proving to be the best idea."

I lied to Troy. I have seen her like this before – not that long ago either. She was like this at the school play when she made her donation to the arts fund. Dave was right then too.

"She needs to see someone. She needs help. You know my mum's a counsellor – maybe she can talk to her," says Troy.

"She has medication. Says she's taking it, but ..."

"Doesn't look like it to me. Giving your gear away, that's crazy stuff."

I get to my feet and kick the dirt. The thread in my stomach pulls tighter. "She's not crazy. Don't say she's crazy?"

Troy backs away from the flying dust. "It's not normal, what she did. She's sick. Mum says that people are born with this sort of stuff. It's not their fault. Just that their brains are wired differently. Like Dr Frankenstein's guy."

I kick the dirt harder. "She's nothing like that. Frankenstein wasn't even real."

"Okay, bad example. But I still reckon I'd be getting her to see someone if I was you."

"You're not me, are you?" I pick up my pack and take off across the asphalt, with Troy's quick steps echoing behind me.

After school I have my second class with Steve Bridges. We talk about how to avoid symmetry in your painting.

Symmetry is what you need in your life, but not in your artwork. I need my life to be even and balanced. But I wonder if it will ever happen. Even when I'm listening to Steve, my mind drifts back to the "Garage Giveaway" and how everything seems to be unravelling and getting more and more out of whack.

Is Mum crazy? Why can't my life be normal for once – with two normal parents in it?

But there's that voice that keeps whispering that maybe Troy and Dad are right.

Face it, Matt. Admit the truth. She's stopped taking her medication.

Chapter Twenty

Troy comes around after I get back from town. Neither of us says anything about the fight at school. It's like it never happened.

I make nachos and lemon cordial, and we sit at the kitchen table getting ready to start our Science assignment.

"Luckily, your mum never got a chance to give this away," Troy pats the kitchen table. "Or we'd have to do our homework on the floor."

"Shut up, will you?" I slam my books on the table.

"Sorry. It was a joke."

"Wasn't funny."

"I guess not." Troy stands and goes to the window. "Hey, what's that yelling?" he asks. "Sounds like a massive argument."

We peer out. Mum and Dad are facing off against each other on the front step – in public, for everyone to see! Great. Why not just tell the whole world how stuffed my family is? Put it on the internet or broadcast it over the radio?

"You have no right to touch our things," yells Dad.

I should have figured he'd react badly to the Garage Giveaway

"I don't know what your problem is. Those suits wouldn't fit you now anyway."

Dad's face goes a deeper shade of red. "That's not the point. They belong to me. They weren't yours to sell."

"I didn't sell them, I gave them away."

"Whatever! They weren't yours to do anything with."

"They're just possessions," Mum says coolly. "They can be replaced." She talks as if she hasn't done anything wrong – or unusual.

Dad's face goes a shade of purple. "How? With what money?"

"Mine."

"Didn't think the invalid pension paid that well." Dad drips sarcasm.

"For your information, I live off my paintings. I don't take charity."

"You just give it." Dad is still talking loudly, but doesn't seem so angry any more. As if he's just realised there's no point to this argument. "You'd better tell me what else you got rid of."

"Just a couple of things of Matt's. He didn't get aggro like you, though."

Dad sighs. "You've been nothing but trouble since you came here. I should never have let you back into our lives."

"It wasn't your choice. Matt wants me here. He's my son."

At that moment, I don't want to be anybody's son. I want to be a worm and slide into a hole in the ground – a really deep dark hole where there's nobody else but me.

"I've had it with you," Dad says. "You've stopped taking your pills again, haven't you?"

I want to block my ears but I don't do it – I have to know the answer. Troy looks as if he doesn't want to be there either.

"So what if I have?" Mum says defensively.

"You promised Matt you'd take them."

Mum's voice wafts back. "I know. But I've been doing so well. I thought I'd just cut back."

"You know it never works when you do that," Dad reminded her.

Mum starts crying. "I just want to paint, that's all. Is that a crime?"

I feel so terrible when she says that. Am I wrong to want her to take tablets so she can be a "normal" mum? Am I trapping her like a caged bird? Clipping her wings so she can't fly away? I want her to choose me, but now she's miserable and she's making everyone else unhappy as well.

Dad doesn't give her any sympathy. "You should have thought about all that before you came here. Do you know what this is doing to your son?"

"Yes." Mum sounds shaky. "I was sure I'd be okay."

"Well, you're obviously not, are you? Maybe you should just leave." Dad's words are clipped and hard.

"Perhaps you're right."

I can't stand it any longer. I run out the front door. "Stop it, both of you!" I yell. "She's my mother and I want her to stay."

"But Matt, it's not working," says Dad.

Mum takes my arm. "I'm so sorry, my darling. I'll do better. I will."

In spite of all the trouble she's caused, I don't want her to go. I've only just found her. I think of what Troy said. "Mum, we can get you some help," I say.

Dad stands watching us, arms crossed.

"I know you can." Mum strokes my arm.

"Please, Dad."

"Doesn't look like I have much choice." He turns away, mumbles under his breath and shuffles off.

When I get back inside Troy's still sitting at the kitchen table. "Maybe you'd be better off without her," he says.

"She's not your mum."

Troy shrugs. We shut our Science books. Neither of us is in the mood for homework. "I guess I'll take off then," says Troy. "We'll try this another time."

"Whatever."

After Troy leaves, Mum walks in the door looking really pleased with herself. "Don't worry about your father. He'll come round. We'll work things out."

I'm not so sure. Why is it impossible for both my parents to be happy at the same time? One is always making sacrifices for the other – and for me.

"But what about your art, Mum? What's going to happen if you can't paint? I heard you telling Dad how much you needed to." And what about the ten grand she promised to the school?

She smiles at me. "I need you more."

I try to sound confident. I have to believe in what I'm saying. "You're right, Mum. We'll work it out. I know we will."

It's Dad I'm maddest with. Why can't he just get over the fact that she's here? He wants her to fail.

———————————————————————

Hey Leonardo,

You can't make people the way you want them to be, not like in a painting.

Is that what painters get from their art, control over their subject?

In a painting, you can give a person a green moustache or orange hair. You can make them appear any way you want. But in real life, you can't control anyone.

It's funny when you're little how your mum and dad seem like they have all the answers.

But now I'm older and I've found out they don't have them either, and what's worse? My parents are the reason for most of my questions.

Matt

Chapter Twenty One

Mum won't answer the door. I know she's there because I can hear her walking up and down the hall.

She's like a tiger I saw at the zoo once. It kept walking back and forth, from one end of its enclosure to the other, going nowhere. It stopped every now and then to press its huge head against the thick glass where all the people were watching. It looked angry and scared. Everyone stepped back from the glass in a single wave of half sighs, half screams. It was as if they knew, and the tiger knew, that it could just put one huge paw through the glass and that would be that. I almost wished it would launch itself at the glass and make a break for freedom.

But Mum's not trapped like that, is she? She *chose* to send me that birthday card. She *chose* to come. I worry about her alone in that house. I worry about what she might do. What am I doing to her?

Troy comes over, and we try and work on our Science assignment again.

Mum brings a batch of chocolate biscuits she baked, walks straight in the front door as if she lives here. "These used to be your father's favourite," she says.

She seems normal. And she did bring biscuits.

"Thanks, Mum. They smell great."

Troy stuffs one in his mouth. "Taste great too," he says, mouth full of biscuit.

Mum smiles. "Thanks, Troy. You can take some for your lunch tomorrow, Matty."

"Thanks, Mum."

"Sorry about the other day. I'm back on my medication and I'm not going off it again, not if it means losing you." She strokes my hair, which is kind of embarrassing in front of Troy, but he doesn't say anything, not even one of his smart comments. Mum has tears in her eyes.

"It's okay, Mum." I take the biscuits from her and eat one.

They're pretty good. "Not sure these will last till tomorrow." I wipe the crumbs off my lips.

Mum smiles. "I'll leave you boys to do your homework," she says. "Talk to you later, Matt. Bye, Troy."

"Bye, Mum."

"See ya." Troy stuffs another biscuit in his mouth.

After Mum leaves, I say, "Looks like things are finally settling down."

Troy raises an eyebrow. "Maybe. Mum says that mental illness isn't that easy to fix. It's not like putting ice on a sprain to make the swelling go down."

"But she's back on her medication ..."

"As long as she keeps taking it."

"She will! Jeez, Troy, what's with you? You never used to be such a downer about everything."

"I'm not. I just don't want to see you get stuffed around again if she goes off her meds."

"She won't."

She wouldn't, would she? She knows that would wreck everything.

Dad walks in from work and sees the biscuits. "Chocolate fudge cookies, my favourite." He pops one into his mouth.

"Yeah, Mum told us."

Dad tenses. "Your mother made these?"

I nod. I think he's going to make some bad comment about her, but he doesn't.

"They're good," he says. "I'm surprised she remembered." He sits at the table and demolishes another biscuit. "So, how's the homework going?"

"Okay," says Troy.

"I'm running low on brain food." I crunch on another biscuit.

"Brain cells more like." Troy laughs.

I pick up my ruler and try to flick him on the shoulder, but he leans back – nearly falling out of his chair. Soon we're chasing each other round the kitchen, and Dad's watching us, laughing.

Hey Leonardo,

Troy and I finally got our Science assignment done. Didn't get a great mark, but with everything going on around here, it's amazing we even got it finished. The Science assignment got me thinking about all the stuff you invented, like clocks and cranes and armoured tanks. You even designed parachutes and flying machines. Man, when did you find the time to do all that? I'm having enough trouble keeping up with school, art classes and family stuff.

And you didn't have computers, or electric paint mixers or cars, or toasters or gas heating, or any of the things that make our life easier today.

I read that when you did your apprenticeship, it took thirteen years. Ours only go for about three or four, and I reckon that's bad enough.

Matt

––––––––––––––––––––––––––––––

Hey Leo,

Just had another lesson with Steve Bridges. It was awesome. I learned how to find the focal point in a painting.

Never really thought about it much before, but there's always one part of a picture that draws your attention first. With your work, it's always the faces, the eyes you painted, that tell so much. Like you really got people, knew what was going on inside their head. I look deeper now, at people's eyes, and try to work out their story – even the ones I don't know. You made me realise I have to understand people If I want to paint them better.

Have been trying this theory on my parents too. Not sure it's working all that well yet. Must be because I know too much backstory already. I guess that gets in the way of gut instinct.

Matt

Chapter Twenty Two

Troy and I usually hang out together on Saturdays but today I'm shopping with Mum. It's like this personal test I set myself when I agreed to go – getting over the memories.

Mum doesn't seem manic at the moment, but I'm still wary about how this will end. At least she's noticed that I'm growing out of everything, which is more than I can say for Dave. Mum only buys me one pair of runners this time. Then we go to a clothes store where she buys me a pair of jeans and a top.

"Can you afford this, Mum?"

"Don't worry, Matt, I'm not going overboard."

I'm relieved when we leave the shopping centre – together – and nothing really weird has gone down.

Next stop is the doctors.

"Hi, Zora, good to see you," says the receptionist. "Doctor will be with you soon."

"Eva, this is my little fella, Matty," she says (even though I'm at least thirty centimetres taller than her).

"Pleased to meet you, Matt."

I can't meet her eyes. *Little fella.* Just when I'm starting to wonder, Mum pipes up and says, "Only joking. Big strapping lad, isn't he?"

Eva nods and turns back to her computer screen. She seems unsure what to say.

I check my phone messages while I wait for Mum, at least she is seeing someone.

She comes out with the doctor, holding a script in her hand. "See, I'm still taking my medication," she says.

We go to the chemist to get her pills then to the pizza shop where Troy and I arranged to meet.

"Might treat myself to a massage. I'll be back to pick you up in a couple of hours." Mum hands me a twenty-dollar note and drives off.

"You two seem to be doing okay," says Troy.

"Yeah, but I think Mum might be getting a bit carried away with the mother/son thing."

"How do you mean?"

"It takes a bit of getting used to. I didn't see her for ten years and now she wants to be my new best friend."

Troy pretends to cry.

I punch him on the shoulder. "As if that's going to happen."

"True. Nobody could live up to my talents, could they?"

Troy puts on his Frankenstein monster face.

Laughing, I bite into the barbecue chicken pizza that's just been delivered to our table.

"I thought you liked having your mum around," Troy says, his mouth full of pizza.

"If she would just give me a bit of space. She's starting to crowd me."

"That gallery opening she took you to last week was pretty awesome."

"Yeah, but it's the doctor's appointments, and shopping and all the other stuff she wants me to do with her – it's a bit much."

"Why don't you talk to her about it?"

"I can't. If I upset her she might leave again." Melted cheese drips from my fingers.

Troy hesitates. "You're fifteen, not five. It's not normal, wanting you to go everywhere with her."

"You only think that because you know she has this bipolar thing."

Troy pushes a pizza crust around the plate. "That's not true!"

"Maybe she just wants to make up for lost time."

Troy puts the crust in his mouth, and talks through cooked pizza chunks. "Yeah, but she needs to get a life."

_____

Hey Leonardo,

I'm starting to think that Mum and I are like your Lady with the Ermine. I'm Mum's pet. Maybe that's all I was to her when I was a kid. Like the Christmas puppy that people buy as an accessory to carry around for everyone to admire – then dump it when it stops being cute and cuddly.

She's definitely suffocating me, wants me with her all the time. Doesn't even seem to care what's going on in my life. If I try to tell her how Mrs D is picking on me or that Troy and I had a fight, she just changes the subject. She makes a big fuss of me, pats me, gives me food then puts me out for the night.

Dad seems to have taken a step back from the action. Troy says he's letting me work things out for myself. I don't mind this new Dave, one who doesn't pick up a book every time there's an issue, one who acts as if he trusts me.

What do think, Leo? If dads can change, surely mums can too?

Matt

Chapter Twenty Three

I'm on the way home from school, when I get a text from Dad: *Meet me @ Mums.*

I show it to Troy. "That's strange. Dad never finishes work early," I say.

Troy shrugs and I get a sick feeling in the pit of my stomach. "Something's wrong. Something's happened."

"Chill," says Troy. "Could be anything. Maybe it's your Mum's birthday."

"Don't think so." I realise I don't actually know when my own mother's birthday is.

My house comes into view from the bus window. There's an ambulance next door. I leap off the bus, jumping all the steps in a single bound.

"Call me," yells Troy out the bus window.

Dad meets me at the front door. I can hear murmuring voices (must be the ambos) coming from the kitchen.

"What's happened?"

"Take it easy, Matt."

"What's happened to Mum? Can I see her?"

Dad speaks carefully, as if he's trying to sound calm. But he's shaking, like he's trying to hold something back. "Don't think that's a good idea just yet. Come and sit down." He walks away from me.

"I don't want to sit down. Tell me what happened."

I follow Dad into the lounge room. We stand across from each other.

"Your mother rang me at work ..."

"Why?"

"She was in the bath and ..."

"And what ... she slipped?" I can't shake the feeling of dread.

Dad's voice is soft. "Matt, there's no easy way to say this, mate, but your mum ... she ... well, she tried to kill herself."

This is bullshit! Why would she do that? We're just starting to work things out. I try to push past him. "I have to see her."

"No, Matt."

Dad seems so in control. I take my fear and anger out on him. "You don't even care."

"Of course I care. But this isn't the first time she's done this sort of thing. It's her way of getting attention."

Dad stands in front of me to block my view, but I catch a glimpse of Mum's dark hair, hanging wet and limp around her face as they take her on a stretcher from the bathroom to the waiting ambulance. I try to run after her, to ask if she's going to be okay. But Dad puts an arm out to stop me.

We follow the ambulance in Dad's car.

I don't talk on the way to the hospital.

"It's not your fault," says Dad.

How does he know?

We wait for two hours in intensive care until the doctor comes. "Is Zora your wife?" he asks Dad.

Dad nods.

So they never got divorced.

"She's going to be okay. Her injuries are not life threatening, but she's going to need psychiatric referral."

"We understand," says Dad.

They won't let us in to see Mum that night, so we go home.

In the morning, we both shuffle down to breakfast with major bags under our eyes. Looks like Dad didn't sleep either.

I put three sugars in my coffee and stir it till Dad says, "You'll wear the bottom out of that mug."

The phone rings, and we both jump. I'm too scared to answer it so Dad picks it up. "Dave Hudson ... yes ... I see ... I think that would be best."

Dad hangs up.

"The hospital?" My voice comes out in a whisper.

Dad nods. "Apparently, your mum is physically okay, but they're moving her to Gardenvale Hospital – to the Acute Psychiatric Unit."

Maybe *I* should ask for a bed there.

Hey Leonardo,

How can you cut through flesh with a knife?

How could you do something like that to yourself – for whatever reason? How could you do it – let yourself bleed into oblivion?

How bad must Mum be feeling to do that?

Matt

Chapter Twenty Four

I take the bus to Gardenvale Hospital. Dad wants to come with me, but I won't let him. He never wanted her back in our lives in the first place.

The hospital is huge and new, not like Barry Hill, at all. In the foyer there are shops where you can buy food and flowers. Damn, I should have brought money. I reckon Mum would have liked flowers.

There's an information desk once you get past the shops. A woman in a blue cardigan asks, "Can I help you, love?"

A lump in my throat makes it hard to get the words out. "I'm ... I'm not sure. I'm ... here to see my mother. Her name's Zora Hudson.

The woman looks up the computer. "Sorry, love. Nobody by that name. Are you sure she's here and not Gardenview, the maternity hospital. Not having a baby, is she? Some people get the two places confused."

Then I remember. "She might be under Matthews," I say.

"Oh, right. Here she is. Room 12. Up the stairs to your left."

"Thanks." I hurry away, wondering if she thinks Mum's mad. Probably the whole world does by now.

As I get closer to room 12, I slow down, not sure if I'm really ready for this. I hesitate outside room 10. The door's open. There's a guy, not that much older than me, sitting on the bed. He's small and wild-looking. When he smiles there are huge gaps between his teeth. "Hi, I'm Kevin."

I'm about to keep walking, when he says, "You want to come in? I never have visitors."

It would be awful, being stuck in a place like this. "Sure." I step into the room.

Kevin bounces up and down. "Sit here." He pats a spot on the moving bed.

"I'm Matt."

Kevin stops bouncing and settles at my feet like a pet dog. "What are you doing here? You don't look crazy. But then you never can tell."

He leaps back onto the bed, rolls up one sleeve of his thin blue pyjama top, and shows me a white line across his wrist. "That's where I slashed last Christmas."

He grabs my hand and makes me feel the fine ridge of his scar.

"It's worse on the other arm. Want to see?"

I shake my head. Kevin pushes his face close to mine till our noses are almost touching, and I can smell his sour breath.

"I'm crazy, you know. Like my mum and my dad and my sister." Kevin's laugh is off-key.

He moves closer when I stand. "Am I scaring you? I scare heaps of people."

I back towards the door. "I'm looking for someone so I'd better go now."

Kevin follows, and grabs my arm. "It's not my fault. It runs in the family."

I try to step outside, but Kevin hangs on. "You can't fight genetics."

"Bye, Kevin." I pull my arm free and run.

I don't stop running till I'm on the bus back to Brabham.

When I get home, Troy is pacing up and down outside my front gate.

He follows me into the house. "So, how'd it go? Did you see her?"

"No."

"Why not?"

I pour us both a glass of milk. "I freaked out. It's a scary place."

Troy grabs the jumper that's tied around his waist and hangs it over his face. He walks around with his arms outstretched. "I am the ghost of Gardenvale," he says in a spooky voice, then collapses laughing.

"Not that kind of scary."

Troy is still laughing when Dad walks in. "What's the joke?" he says.

"Wasn't really that funny anyway." I signal to Troy.

"Gotta go, Mr H. Catch you later."

I grab my backpack and head to my room, slam the door shut before Dad can hassle me about today. I'm too embarrassed to tell him what a wuss I am.

If I hadn't been so freaked out by Kevin, I would have got to see Mum, and I could have asked her stuff. Stuff about us, about me, about genetics, and whether I might be bipolar too.

I lie on the bed, banging my head against the pillow, thinking about Kevin. I never expected to see someone that young in a psych place. Is he right? Is madness something you can get from your parents?

My name is called over the PA, to go to the principal's office. But I don't move. Since I heard what Mum did, I've felt kind of sedated, like I'm living in a haze and nothing's real. Is that what Mum feels like on the medication? No wonder she doesn't want to take it.

"You're in for it, Hudson!" says Carly Ralph.

Damon Knox asks, "What's Marvo Matt done now?"

"Don't listen to them," says Troy.

"I'm not." The words seem to come out of my mouth without me making them. My mind can't focus. How do you forget the image of your mother lying in a bath full of blood? Even though I didn't see her do it, my imagination does a good job of painting the picture for me.

"Matt Hudson to Mr Madden's office now!"

"You'd better go, Matt," says Troy.

"Yeah."

I get to my feet and Troy pushes me towards the door. "Good luck, mate," he whispers.

I stand in front of Mr Madden's antique desk.

"You wanted to see me, sir?"

Madden looks at me intently. "You weren't at school yesterday. Want to tell me about it?"

I glare at him. "Not really."

"Your father rang. He told me your mother had to go to hospital. It might help to talk," says Madden. He has that same

140

"I'm here to help you" look that Dave wears.

"I doubt it." Talking about it isn't going to fix anything. I bite my lip. Crap. If I try and say anything I'm going to howl – right then and there in Madden's office.

"It's not your fault, Matt. Your mother's ill. It's not anyone's fault."

What would he know? I'm so sick of people trying to tell me who I should be and how I should feel.

I slam out of the headmaster's office. My anger's too big to fit inside my body. It's like the day I found out Mum wasn't really dead. I run, want to keep running and never stop.

Finally, when I'm out of breath, I collapse on the ground and lie facedown on the soft grass next to the river. The sun beats down on the back of my head, but I don't care if I die of sunstroke. And nobody else will either.

Troy finds me before the sun has a chance to fry me.

"Hey, Matt! There you are." He flops down on the grass. "Madden got me out of class to look for you. Thanks for that," he says with a grin.

"Any time."

"What happened?"

"He wanted to talk about Mum. Dad phoned him. Madden reckons it's not my fault she did it to herself. But that's crap." The grass itches my face. I sit up.

Troy rolls a blade of grass between his palms. "What does your dad say?"

"He reckons she just wants attention. Says she's nothing but trouble. I hate him."

Troy hesitates. "He's got a point, you know."

"Whose side are you on anyway?"

"I'm *your* friend, trying to help you sort through all this."

I get up. "Well, you're not helping. So leave me alone."

Troy stands too. "You have to face it. Your life has been a train wreck since she came on the scene. She's stuffed in the head and she's making you the same way. I know it's not her fault, but you can't let her drag you into her crazy world."

"Don't call her crazy!" The anger bulges inside me. I'm mad with so many people: Dad for lying in the first place; Mum for doing this to herself and now Troy's giving me a hard time as well. It's too much. I can't hold it in any more. I take a wild swing.

Troy sidesteps my clenched fist, but the blow catches him on the side of the face and sends him into the river. His face goes under, his arms and legs flail about.

At first I think it's just another one of his jokes. But he's not coming up. I dive in, lurch about until I grab hold of his arm, drag him to the surface and swim to the bank. He's still a bit dazed, but manages to cough up the water he swallowed.

I feel worse than ever. Troy's my best mate, the one who stuck by me through all this – and I nearly drowned him.

"I'm sorry, Troy." What else can I say?

Troy smiles weakly. "No harm done." His voice is croaky.

"You're right! My life's a train wreck. I just don't know what to do about it."

We lie on the grass, drying in the sun.

I sit up. "Troy, do you think I'm like her?"

"Course you are. She's your mother."

"That's not what I mean. Do you reckon I'm moody?"

"No more than anyone else I know."

Troy looks at me. For once he's not laughing. "What are you really asking?"

I take a deep breath. Force out the words that I've not had the guts to say out loud. "Do you reckon I could have this bipolar thing? It's supposed to run in families."

"Nah, you're not bipolar. Not that I really know much about it. But you seem normal to me. Hot-headed and stubborn maybe, but not crazy. What does your dad say?"

"Haven't asked him."

"Maybe your mum can help you. She'd know better than anyone what the signs are."

_____

Hey Leonardo,

Every time I look at one of your paintings, I realise it's the truth and the detail that make your work so great.

You never seemed to paint anything without looking into it. No surface sketches for you.

I think that's what I love about your Drapery Study. I never thought of clothes as having a life of their own – but they do. We all wear an outer layer to hide who we really are.

Matt

_____

Hey Leonardo,

You once said that "The desire to know is natural to all good people."

Mind you, I'm not saying I'm a good person – just that I need to know.

Ever since she sent me that card, I've wanted to find out more, to know all of it.

Gotta go back and see Mum. Face this head-on. Have to live with whatever happens.

Matt

Chapter Twenty Five

It takes me three days to summon the courage to go back to the hospital – seventy-two hours of fighting myself. Should I or Shouldn't I? Troy offers to come but this is something I have to do alone.

"Be careful." He punches me lightly on the arm as we walk to the bus stop.

"I will. I can't believe that we're still friends, after I nearly drowned you," I say.

Troy laughs. "You won't get rid of me that easily."

"I gave it a good go."

"Yeah, but you got me out in the end. Besides, I guess I asked for it." He points to the side of his face, which is still bruised from where I punched him. "You know this big mouth of mine. It's always getting me into trouble."

"Good luck," he says as I hop on the bus to Gardenvale.

Walking up the hallway to Mum's room, I think about what Troy said. Mum's the one who can tell me if I'm bipolar or not.

She's resting when I walk in. "Hi, darling, I'm glad you came." Her voice is thin and dry like the air-conditioned room. She pats the bed. "Sit down and talk to me," she says.

She's wearing a faded blue hospital gown and looks so unlike herself – colourless. I made this happen. I should have left Mum alone with her peppercorn trees and stray cats, back in Hillton in her world where she creates unbelievable paintings.

There are bars on the windows. Do they really need to be there?

"I'm sorry, Mum." I bend to kiss her.

She strokes my hair. "It's not your fault, Matt. It never was."

I lay my head on her shoulder. "But look at you, Mum. You don't belong here."

"It's okay, really. They look after me."

A nurse comes in and hands Mum a couple of pills that she swallows without water. "I need professional help," she says.

"You seem okay now."

Mum shakes her head. "That's the medication. They've got me on some pretty strong stuff."

I look away. "Mum, do you think I could be bipolar?"

She seems really stunned by my question. "Why would you think that?"

"I get pretty angry sometimes."

Mum makes me face her. "Lots of people get angry. I wouldn't worry, Matty. You seem fine. I know I'm not a great one to judge, but there are so many things about being bipolar that you just don't seem to be."

"Like what?"

"Insomnia for starters. You don't seem to have any trouble sleeping."

I think of all the times Dad has to wake me up for school because I slept through my alarm. "Yeah, I guess you're right about that."

"Do you think about dying a lot? Because I do."

"Not really."

I hardly ever think about the fact that my own life's going to end one day. In fact, the only death I've thought about much at all has been Mum's – and it turned out she wasn't dead after all.

"Ever get the feeling you can't slow down, no matter how you try?"

I think about that day I bolted out of Madden's office, but even then I got so tired I had to rest. "No."

Mum smiles. "I'm no medical expert. I'm not even always in my right mind. But you don't seem to have a problem to me."

I put my hand in hers. "What about you, Mum? Will you be okay?"

"Sure I will. I'm a tough cookie, you know. I have to be."

I've never thought of her as tough. She always seems so vulnerable to me. But then again, to live without your kid for his sake for ten years must have taken some guts.

"When you come back, I'm going to look after you."

Mum places a hand on either side of her, as if she's propping herself up. "I'm not coming back, Matt. I'm going home."

"But you're okay if you stay on your medication."

"I'm sorry, Matt. I just can't do it. I made a decision once before, and it was the right one. I'm better off away from people, where I can't hurt them."

"But what about us?"

Mum's firm. "You were doing all right till I came back into your life. Seems to me things went downhill from there."

I try to hold back the tears.

"I'll write," says Mum. "And maybe you can come and stay sometimes, if you're game?"

At least she's not going completely out of my life again. I'll still have a mother. "That'd be good, Mum."

She takes my hand again. "I'm really sorry, Matt."

She's not the one who should be sorry. She can't help the way she is. "It was my fault all this happened, Mum."

Mum smiles. "Don't blame yourself, Matty. It was my choice to come and I'm glad I made it, glad I got to know you."

I slip my arms around her.

"I'm sorry I can't be the person you want me to be," she whispers.

"You're still my mum."

On the way home, I'm more relaxed than I have been in ages. The thread in my stomach is looser. Everything's out in the open now, there are no more secrets.

Back home, Troy is waiting for me. I wince at the huge bruise still on his cheek from where I hit him.

"Jeez, your face looks awful."

"Don't worry," says Troy. "It's a real chick magnet."

Trust Troy to make a joke of it. "Girls find *that* attractive?"

"Well, maybe not. But I've been getting plenty of attention – from Tina Armstrong, in particular."

"Serious?"

"Yeah, I told her you walloped me, but she didn't believe me. Thinks it was my old man, but I'm too afraid to tell. I heard her talking to Josie Walker about it."

I laugh. "So, she's giving you plenty of sympathy, is she?"

"Yeah."

"Poor you!"

"Don't worry. I can handle it. Tina told me if ever I need to talk to someone, she's happy to listen. Even gave me her phone number."

I shake my head in disbelief.

"So, how did you go?" asks Troy.

"Okay. I'll tell you all about it tomorrow. You'd better go and send your girlfriend a text."

———————————————

Hey Leonardo,

I read how you used to buy those birds in the marketplace then open their cages so they could fly away. I thought it was amazing. Now I'm going to try to be just like you.

I'm going to give Mum back her freedom.

I'm letting her go.

Dad reckons it will be "best for all of us".

Matt

Chapter Twenty Six

Mum's gone, and life has slowed down again. It's not so chaotic. I don't get up every morning feeling like I'm being torn in two.

Dad drops me at art class. While I wait for Steve to finish serving his last customer for the day, I lay out my paints and brushes.

"Today, we're moving on to formal composition," Steve says.

I'm starting to think art classes might not work for me after all. I just want to paint.

Steve asks, "Have you seen Leonardo's *Virgin of the Rocks*?"

I nod. I've committed every Leonardo da Vinci masterpiece to memory.

"It's based on triangles – a common compositional device used by artists today."

"So? Can't we just paint?"

Steve waves a brush at me. "Patience, Matt. Leonardo spent thirteen years perfecting his craft – ask your mum, she'll tell you."

"I know already. I read it in a book about him."

Steve smiles. "Learning to paint takes time."

"Mum went back to Hillton."

"Oh."

A week later Troy and I catch the bus home from school to my place.

Troy pats me on the back. "I owe you big-time for that bruise," he says. "The delectable Ms Armstrong and I have never been friendlier."

Troy and I haven't seen much of each other lately. He's been over at Tina's place a lot, getting help with his homework, and moral support for his supposedly tragic life.

When we get to my house, Mum's car's in the driveway. I go hot then cold – icy, goose bump cold. I haven't seen her since the hospital. What's she doing here? Is she okay?

Troy groans when he sees her car. "Great! She's back."

"You wait here. I'll talk to her. Find out what she wants," I say.

"Fine," says Troy. "Just don't get sucked in by her, all right?"

"She's not that bad."

Troy shrugs. "Be careful, Matt. Don't let her hurt you."

As soon as I walk into the house, I know something's wrong. Mum's in there. I'm sure of it. But there's something else drowning out the thick sweet scent of her perfume. It's smoke!

I open the kitchen door. Everything has been taken from the cupboards, piled into the middle of the kitchen floor and set alight. The house is on fire.

Mum is standing there, throwing more stuff onto the flames.

"Hi, Matty," she says calmly, as if what she's doing is perfectly normal. She smiles like Mona Lisa. As if she's found the secret to life and the universe. "To make it work for us, we have to burn the past. Then we can start a brand-new future together."

I can't get near the sink, the flames are too high.

"Mum, get out before you get hurt!"

"Don't be silly, Matty. Everything will to be fine." She goes to the door. "I'm just going to get more stuff."

It makes me think back to the time when I burned Dad's book. Still, I knew exactly what I was doing then. Mum doesn't. In her world, burning down our house is going to fix everything. I know it won't.

I race to the laundry, fill two buckets with water and throw them on the flames. The fire flickers, but doesn't go out. It has taken hold in the cupboard next to the dishwasher and is making its way up the wall.

I whip out my phone, and call the fire brigade. Then I run back to the kitchen with two more buckets of water.

Mum walks in with Dave's squash trophy in one hand and my laptop in the other.

I grab them from her and race out the front door.

"Here, mind these," I say to Troy, and run back into the house without any explanation.

Mum has more gear in her hands. "You'll see, Matty. This will fix everything." She tosses some of Dave's books into the burning kitchen. Mum doesn't seem to notice the heat from the flames. She walks straight to them like a moth to a light. The fire is all up one wall and the overhead cupboards are sagging dangerously.

Mum steps back to look at what she's done – just like Troy and I did at the water tank on Mather's Hill. *Mum's proud to be destroying our house.* She has this insane smile, as if this will bring her inner peace, as if it's the solution she's been looking for all her life.

"Watch out!" I yell.

The overhead cupboard slides down the wall and falls. One corner hits Mum on the head, knocking her sideways into the middle of the burning pile. It all happens so fast.

She's lying where she fell, no sound, no screams, just her still body in the flames. I grab her from the fire. Fear gives my whole body a jolt. My throat is dry. This can't be happening.

I carry Mum to the lounge room and roll her over and over to put out the flames. Her pulse is weak. She's out cold but she still has that stupid smile on her face.

She's not very big, but she's a dead weight when I lift her and sling her over my shoulder. I run from the house screaming, "Help! Somebody, help! Fire! Help!" My voice is high and scared. I lay Mum carefully on the grass, well away from the house, take off my jacket and put it under her head for a pillow. There's a black patch on her temple, but I don't know if it's a bruise from when the cupboard fell on her or soot from the fire. Smoke and flames are rearing out of the chimney. I reach for my mobile to call an ambulance, but the phone's not in my pocket. It must have fallen out inside. I look towards the house. The laptop and trophy are still on the front verandah. Where's Troy? Why didn't he stay where I left him?

Running through the front door, through the haze of smoke, I see Troy down the end of the hallway. He must have gone around the back looking for me. I think he's calling my name, but I can't be sure over the roar of the fire. I see him framed by a burning doorway. I hear sirens. I see Troy put his arms above his head for protection, hear him scream as the roof collapses.

Strong hands drag me back, away from him. "Troy!" I shout his name. But they won't let me go to him.

Two firefighters half-drag, half-carry me outside. The other one goes back for Troy.

Next thing I remember is waking up in the ambulance. The pain in my arms is worse than anything I've felt before. "Troy!" I whisper through dry lips. "Is my friend okay?"

"We'll let you know as soon as we hear something." The paramedic is a woman about Mum's age but so different. She's tall and blond with big arms, and her voice is firm and strong when she speaks. She smiles into my eyes, calmly strokes my hair and tells me, "Try and relax, Matt. You're going to be fine."

Chapter Twenty Seven

When I open my eyes, I think I'm still in the ambulance. But the roof is too high and nothing is moving. There are no tyre sounds on bitumen road, or flickering traffic lights whizzing past. No siren, just the sound of my own breathing, and feet walking towards me on a hard floor.

My arms hurt – a lot. A woman is standing over me. "Mum?" My voice comes out thin and soft, like it hasn't been used for a while. I close my eyes again.

Of course it's not Mum. She died when I was five, didn't she? Something's not right.

I open my eyes again – slowly – first my right eye, then my left. I exhale with relief. I'm not crazy. This woman is nothing like Mum. She's tall with lighter hair and a dark blue cardigan, not Mum's colour at all. But how would I know that if she died when I was small? I'm so confused. I close my eyes again. It's safer in the darkness.

"You're awake?"

That's a voice I know. I peer through half-closed eyelids at Dad. I want to open my eyes again, but I'm having trouble working out what's real. Maybe all of this is a dream.

I close my eyes tighter, and the orange screen behind my lids goes darker. In my head, I see an old man with white hair and a beard wearing a strange-looking beret. The man's eyebrows are shaped like a "~" on a computer keyboard – can't remember what that thing's called. In one hand, the man holds a paintbrush which he brandishes like a weapon. He throws his words at me, "Art is never finished, only abandoned."

I don't understand. I don't get any of this.

"The truth of things is the chief nutriment of superior intellects," he says.

Truth. Somehow, I know that's important to both of us. Who is he? Grandfather? Wizard? Leonardo? Where did that last thought come from?

I don't know whether to open my eyes or keep them closed. Don't know what's real. There are more footsteps. My arms still hurt – and my chest is heavy, like a weight is pressing down on it.

I reach out desperately and touch Dad's face. The pain shooting through my fingers makes me wince. That's definitely real. I open my eyes.

Dad pulls away.

A man in a white coat asks, "How are you feeling, Matt?"

How does he know my name? I close my eyes and head back to the darkness.

"It's all right, Matt." His voice is calm. "I'm Doctor Fredrikson."

A doctor – that information helps.

I open my eyes again.

The doctor smiles. "You've been out of it for a few days now, Matt. It takes a while to reorient yourself."

How do I get rid of this burning smell in my nostrils? And the taste of smoke?

If my throat didn't hurt so much, I think I'd scream in frustration. I look at my bandaged hands and wonder what's under the wadding.

The clunk of wheels on hard floor makes me try to turn my head to look, but everything hurts.

"Here's your lunch, Matt." A woman with dark eyes and a big smile stands beside the bed, holding a bowl on a silver tray.

She knows me too?

Dad takes the food from her and places it on a table next to me.

The clunking wheels and footsteps disappear.

I stare at my bandaged hands. Dad and the woman in the blue cardigan (she says she's a nurse) take one arm each and help raise me up to almost sitting. It makes me dizzy.

Once my stomach has settled and the room stops spinning, Dad says, "Let's have a go at lunch."

"Lunch?"

"Nothing too hard – it's soup." He dips the spoon into the bowl. "Open up."

I open my mouth as wide as I can, but my lips feel as if they are cracking. Dad spoons in cold soup. I can't taste it, and it hurts my throat when it goes down. The pain makes it hard to breathe. I panic and push the spoon away. Soup spills everywhere.

That woman is still there – the first one in the blue cardigan. The one I thought was my mother.

"Try and stay calm," she says. "It's important that you eat something."

"Everything's going to be fine, Matt," says Dad.

Is it? It's hard to breathe, hard to swallow and even harder to talk.

The nurse gets a cloth and wipes pale yellow soup from the white sheet. On my left is another bed with exactly the same sheets on it.

"You're in hospital." Dad holds my face gently between his hands, stops my darting eyes.

That explains the doctor and nurse.

Doctor Fredrikson comes back after lunch.

"I'm going to need to check those arms, I'm afraid," he says.

I close my eyes. Don't want to know what's under there. I try and get the old man with the deep voice back in my head – Leonardo.

When the bandages come off and the air hits my arms, the pain is almost too much.

Help me, Leonardo!

The old man is back. He waves his paintbrush at me. "The noblest pleasure is the joy of understanding."

Wish I understood.

The old man fades. The bandages are back on. I open my eyes. Doctor Fredrikson sits on the chair next to my bed. His eyes pan from Dad to me, like a lighthouse beacon.

"I'm afraid I have bad news, Matt," he says.

What does that mean?

As Dad turns away, I see a tear in the corner of his eye.

"The left arm is healing well."

What's wrong with it anyway?

"But I think we may have to operate on your right arm. We don't want you to lose the use of it, do we?"

I shrug. None of it means much to me. Everything's happening all out of order. I'm still not sure if any of this is real.

Dad smiles. "We can't have that, can we?" he says. "Can't have anything stop you from painting, from being the next Leonardo da Vinci."

I start vomiting and can't stop. The pain's unbearable. It's like someone ripping out my insides. Leonardo da Vinci – that's who the old man is!

Suddenly, I know for sure that Nurse Blue Cardigan is *not* my mother. The smell of vomit temporarily overpowers the smell of smoke.

I try to shut down my brain, but random thoughts spew out like lava.

Dad watches helplessly as Nurse Blue Cardigan rubs my back and swaps the bucket for a clean one when she needs to.

But no matter what she does, I don't feel clean. Sweat pours out of me.

My memory has returned. And I remember everything. "Troy. What happened to Troy?"

Chapter Twenty Eight

Doctor Fredrikson glances at Dad and nods.

"Troy. What happened?" My memory is splintered with snapshots. Troy ... the roof ... running. "Did he ... is he ...?" I can't say it. Can't say the word.

Dad sits on the bed and rests a hand on my shoulder. "We're very hopeful he'll recover. But he's not there yet I'm afraid."

"His burns were severe," the doctor says softly.

"How severe?" My voice is high pitched and my throat stings with the effort of forcing the words out so loud. This is my fault! I'm the idiot who went looking for my mother. "Where is he? Can I see him?"

"He's very heavily sedated," Doctor Fredrikson stands.

"I have to see him!"

Doctor Fredrikson is talking to Nurse Blue Cardigan. I'm not sure he heard me.

"I need to see Troy."

Dad nods, but doesn't say anything.

The doctor comes back. "We've arranged a chair for you. But you'll also have to gown up. We can't risk infection.

To Troy or me? I don't really care. I just want to see him. Need to see him. "I'll do whatever it takes."

The doctor runs his hand down his chin. "It's going to hurt."

Gowning up or seeing Troy? "Let's do it." I put my bandaged hands on the arms of the chair to try and pull myself up, but the pain makes me yell out.

"We can take care of it." Nurse Blue Cardigan lays her hand gently on my back like she's trying to siphon away the pain.

She helps me into a plastic-coated gown, drapes it over me carefully and does it up. Tries not to come in contact with me, and cause more pain. She slips the hat on, but gloves won't fit over my bandaged hands. Before we enter burns ICU, Nurse BC slips a mask over my face.

Troy is lying in his hospital bed, not moving. He's wrapped in layers of white sterile dressing like I'm wearing on my hands. It goes all up his arms and around his chest though. He's too still and quiet. This isn't Troy. It's someone I don't know. I will him to leap out of bed. To slap me on the back, grinning. To say, "Hey Matty Boy. Got you a good one then didn't I?" Then I'd know he was Troy. Then I could breathe normally again.

His arms are in splints, stiff like Frankenstein. Troy would love the irony, but it cuts me like a knife. I wish we could go back, all of us. I wish we could go back to before Mum. I wish we could go back to Troy and I painting together. Now neither of us can hold a can let alone press the spray nozzle.

"Will he be able to paint again?" I turn to Dad.

He shrugs. "I honestly don't know. His arms were badly burnt, and his chest."

I can see that for myself.

It's so hot in here. I'm sweating, and so is Troy. His face is shiny with it. His almost unscathed face. It's the only part that still looks like him, but it doesn't have his spark. Troy put his arms up when the roof caved. I wonder if that's what saved him.

A nurse comes to move him. He is so gentle with Troy, but it still has to hurt. Troy groans, but doesn't wake up.

I've had grafts, but they're nothing in comparison to what Troy must have had. No wonder he's sedated almost into a coma. So much pain.

In the corridor on the way back to my room, we see Troy's family.

Troy's mum bends to kiss me on the cheek. "Good to see you Matt. How are you doing?"

"Never better." I bite my tongue. Dumb thing to say when Troy's lying in his hospital bed looking like shit. But it's the sort of comment he would make.

Troy's mum crouches in front of the wheel chair. "I'm glad Matt. None of this is your fault you know."

"He went in looking for me. He tried to save me ... and now look at him."

Tina steps forward. "And you would have done the same for him."

I don't know that for sure. I never got the chance. The fire fighters pulled me back.

Tina rests her hand lightly on mine and looks into my eyes. "He's going to be okay. This is Troy we're talking about."

"Yeah." If anyone can bring Troy back, it's Tina.

Chapter Twenty Nine

A week later, Doctor Fredrikson signs my release. I can't wait to bust out of here, but I feel like a traitor leaving Troy. There's still rehab to do, and I'll have regular dressing changes, and more grafts, but for now I'm going home.

As we drive out of the hospital car park, I remember that we don't have a home anymore, not till the insurance company rebuilds it. Dad rented us a unit a few streets away.

"Can we stop in and see Steve Bridges?" I ask as we cruise past the art shop.

"Sure." Dad does a u-turn and pulls into a parking spot right out the front.

Steve Bridges flinches when he sees my arms bandaged like a mummy, but he forces a smile. "Great to see you, Matt."

"I'm not coming back to class," I tell him. Painting is what made Mum stop taking her meds. Painting is where all this started, back when I was five and Mum first went off her pills because they stopped her from painting.

"You're not your mother," says Steve. "Don't turn your back on your art. That's what defines who you are – not the people you were born to, not genes or family resemblances. It's the essence of you."

Maybe he's right, and maybe I'll pick up a paintbrush again, but there doesn't seem any point to it, even if my arms heal, and even optimistic Doctor Fredrikson isn't making any guarantees about that.

Being able to pick up anything is impossible for now, I can't even write with my keyboard. I have to rely on the voice recognition software on my laptop getting it right. Lucky for me, most of the time it does.

Our house is gone. There's not one part of my life my mother hasn't wreaked havoc on. I wish I hadn't made her come here. I wish she'd stayed a hazy memory.

"You can't blame yourself," says Dad. "None of this is your

fault." He's got no books left so whatever he says comes from the heart of Dave Hudson, not the pen of a self-help guru.

Hey Leonardo,

I need you to help me understand. How could Mum have done it? How can your brain be that twisted?

I get Dad now, and his whole protection thing. I reckon if I'd looked at your Dreyfus Madonna – really looked sooner, I might have understood. The way she's holding that baby – it looks so fragile.

But that's because babies are fragile – and little kids – that's why Dad needed to protect me from my own mother.

I'm not a baby now. I'm hurt and I'm changed, but not fragile. I'm going to get through this for Troy. I'm going to save myself. She can't do any worse to me. I can't do any worse to myself.

Some mistakes just can't be undone, Leo.

Matt

Chapter Thirty

A week later, I'm lying on the couch with the television on, flickering in and out of sleep.

The doorbell rings and Dad goes to answer it. I close my eyes again. It won't be for me.

"Hey sleepy head." A pillow lands on my chest.

"Tina?"

"That's me."

Fear fills my chest instead of air. I can't breathe. "Troy?" It comes out like a squeak. "Is he okay?"

She grins. "He woke up. He's got a long road ahead. Lots of surgery and rehab, but he's not a quitter."

"And he's got you."

Her grin widens. "I guess he has. He is cool, just like you told me when we went to the National Gallery that time. You just have to look past the jokes."

"Yeah."

Her face goes serious. "And now I can't wait for him to start cracking them again."

"Me too."

Hey Leonardo,

Ironic how my laptop was saved and Dad's old squash trophy, but not the important stuff. Troy's arms are still a mess, and he's got months of surgery ahead of him.

I printed off all those letters I wrote to you before the fire and gave them to Mrs D today. She was rapt.

"Thought I was never going to see these," she said.

Probably wouldn't have shown her except there's no point in keeping them to myself now.

Mum and what she did is newspaper headlines again, so my life is out in the open for everyone to read about.

You know what it's like to be notorious, Leo. You made headlines because of the way you chose to love. I guess in a way, Mum's the same.

It's hard being back at school. Nobody knows what to say. Tomorrow I get an aide to scribe for me until my hands get better.

I can still work on the computer because it has voice activation, so I talk, and it writes down what I say. See, my world is very different from the one you lived in.

I can't carry the laptop to class. Can't carry anything yet.

At least when the aide comes, I won't have to look at Troy's empty chair all day.

Matt

Chapter Thirty One

Dad stands across the kitchen bench from me. "While you're at school today, I'm going to visit your mum."

"Why?" Why should she get out of all this without an aftermath?

"She doesn't have anyone else. And she's hurting too."

I can't look at him. "I don't see why she should have it easy when you look at what she did to us," I say to Dad.

"Matt, I know you're angry with her. I know she's done terrible things, but don't let the anger eat away at you. It will only cause you more pain. Your mother's sick. She never meant to hurt anyone."

"Well, she did!" I sip on my banana smoothie, the breakfast I can eat without being spoon fed. Automatically, I go to stir it with my straw, but the pain makes me stop.

"Matt, her life has never been easy. She's not evil, she's just a person with a sickness she can't help."

I'm working on trying to feel compassion for her, but I'm not there yet. The weird thing is that the person I'm doing it for is Troy. It's what he would want. Troy is always in my head with his lopsided grin, and his voice like a fairground ride – the quick up-and-down way he has of talking. Troy was always so excited to be living and being and doing. I miss his rainbow coloured voice – bending light and making everything spectacular. I need to hear him speak. To tell me that he's okay, that we all will be.

Hey Leonardo,

I think I'm really doing this for you. To finish it! I'm not going to leave sketchy lines that don't have definition. Things shouldn't be left unsaid. I guess that's one of our differences, Leo. I reckon things have to be complete – no matter how difficult it is to apply the last coat.

It was different for you though – with your paintings, I mean. You always had so many things on the go and you never thought your works were finished, even when everyone else did. You were such a perfectionist, everything had to be just right. But if there's one thing I've learned from all this, it's that life isn't that simple. A few brushstrokes just won't make things right.

It's been a while since it happened but it doesn't seem like it. I feel like there's never going to be a time when it's not new and terrible and unreal, when I don't have this sick feeling in my stomach, remembering.

But you need to finish things. It's the only hope you have of moving on. And that's what I have to do. I've seen what happens when you get stuck in the past. It's what made Mum do what she did.

Dad forgives Mum. He says it isn't her fault that her brain is wired wrong. Dad wired our trailer back to front once. When you put your foot on the brake, the blinkers started flashing and when you put the blinker on, the brakelight came on. Dad changed the connections around and the problem was fixed.

Not so easy to do that with a brain.

You said that the learning you get when you're young, "Arrests the evil of old age." Yeah, well it sucks. If this is the sort of learning I have to do, then I'd rather not grow old.

I guess this letter is for our sake as well – for Troy and me – to help me understand and move on.

Matt

We're in the new house. The rebuilt one. The one where our old house used to be. It's new and white, and the verandah doesn't sag and the roof tin doesn't rattle.

I'm glad it's different. We're all different. But mostly, I think we're going to be okay.

"I've got something to show you guys." Dad leads us around to the driveway.

"Great, it's the side of a house," says Troy.

Tina laughs. She seems to think that everything he says is funny these days. He's not quite back to form, but he's getting there.

"Not just any side of the house," says Dad. "Wait here." He points to chairs lined up in a row.

He goes into the garage and comes back with the wheelbarrow full of brushes and paint.

"Go for it guys," he says. "This is your mural wall."

I sit stunned, but Troy is right onto it. He uses his chin to push himself forward in his motorised chair.

Tina opens the tin ... bright green ... Troy's favourite. She plucks out a paintbrush and holds it out to Troy. He grabs it in his mouth, dips it in the tin and starts painting.

His style is different now. A brush is not the same as a can, but you can get even finer detail.

"Troy, you're awesome!"

"I know." He grins back, and the paint brush drops out of his mouth, flicks green paint all over the new concrete driveway.

I glance at Dad, hold my breath.

He laughs. "Guess we might as well paint that too."

Troy nods and paint flicks everywhere.

I watch fascinated as Troy's picture starts to take shape. He swaps brushes and goes for different colors. It's Venice. He's painting Venice. He nods at me and I pick up a brush and start working on the high parts of the wall.

It's not the water tank and we don't have cans, but we're Matt and Troy again. Two guys painting together, just like Leonardo and Verrocchio.

———————————————

Hey Leo,

So you see, Leo, I'm back painting again. Like Steve Bridges said, it's part of who I am.

There has been a lot of comment in town about our mural wall.

Steve likes the new painting too. Reckons it's our best work yet. (Mind you, he always says that.) For the first time ever he agrees with PC Huggins. "It's much more relevant. Your art has really matured over the last twelve months," he says.

Life does that to you, Leo, doesn't it? Whether you want it or not, life drags you forward.

Matt

Dad and I talk a lot about what happened, about Mum mostly, and how there are just some things you can't control.

He says there have been some positives in all the suffering.

"Like what?" I ask. "What are the positives?"

My hands are almost healed, and we're washing the dishes in our new kitchen, where everything is new. "At least we now have a frying pan that works," says Dave.

Never thought that being able to wash dishes was something I'd ever aspire to. "Getting you new suits was a good thing too."

Dad pretends to be offended. "Steady on," he says. "They were the height of fashion in their day."

"When was that, the 1800s?"

Dad laughs. "Don't you be cheeky?"

He grabs a tea towel and chases me around the kitchen of our new house.

I stay just out of reach.

Suddenly, I stop, thinking of the times Troy and I did this in our old kitchen.

Dad put his arms around me. "You couldn't have stopped her, Matt. Nobody could have."

"I'm sorry about your book, Dad, the one I burned."

He cuffs me gently. "I think it had probably had its day, like the suits, don't you?"

Things between Dad and me are back to what they were – only different. None of us could have stayed the same after everything that happened.

Hey Leonardo,

We were both right.

People can come from such different places and still be right.

People don't have to be the same – they don't even have to know each other to think the same.

And sometimes you come from people who are not like you at all. And sometimes you're lucky enough to meet someone in your life who really knows you and is your friend in spite of who you are.

I still believe that truth is more important than anything. But you have to know how to handle it. And when stuff happens, you can't begin to dissect it and put your life back together until you find out the whole truth of it.

This is it from me, Leo.

I turned sixteen today and Dad bought me a brand-new easel. No surprise letters – no word from Mum. Dad's taking Troy, Tina and me to the gallery for my birthday, to look at a "People in Oils" exhibition.

Can't wait! But you know what Leo, whenever I look at a portrait of a lady, I'll still be comparing it to a da Vinci.

Dad's calling. It's time to switch off, pull the plug – time to put away my laptop. Time to go.

This is all I have left to say.

Bye, Leo and thanks for everything.

Matt

www.ingramcontent.com/pod-product-compliance
Lightning Source LLC
Chambersburg PA
CBHW071224290326
41931CB00037B/1957